The Education of an Editor

The Education
of an Editor

BURROUGHS MITCHELL

DOUBLEDAY & COMPANY, INC.
GARDEN CITY, NEW YORK
1980

Grateful acknowledgment is made for the use of the poem "Stony Beach" from *New and Selected Things Taking Place*, copyright © 1954 by May Swenson. Permission granted by Little, Brown & Company.

Library of Congress Cataloging in Publication Data

Mitchell, Burroughs.
   The education of an editor.

   1. Mitchell, Burroughs.   2. Editors—United States
—Biography.   I. Title.
PN149.9.M5A33   070.4′092′4 [B]

ISBN: 0-385-15032-6
Library of Congress Catalog Card Number 79–7204

For Jean

Contents

Author's Note

This book consists of patches of reminiscence, literary appreciation, portraiture, and reflection. I have written about some writers I have known well and about a few other people, like Maxwell Perkins, who have been intimately connected with the writing life. This is not an autobiography, nor an explication of book publishing (called by the British publisher Frederick Warburg, with some irony, "An Occupation for Gentlemen"). A number of fine writers, friends of mine, do not appear here because I have limited myself to the books and authors who support some points I've tried to make about my editorial education.

Gloria Jones must bear the responsibility for my writing the book. She got me into it. She was abetted by my wife Jean, by Willie Morris, and eventually by Sandy Richardson of Doubleday, who saw better than I the course the book should take. Jean has had to suffer with a beginning writer accustomed to other writers' problems but not to his own. She has also given me sharp professional advice on the manuscript.

I want to express my gratitude to Helen Mitchell, who lived through many of the experiences recorded here. Our son Bruee also lived through some of them, apparently without damage.

I am of course deeply indebted to Charles Scribner's Sons and to the two Charles Scribners who employed me. The firm was for thirty years the location of my editorial life.

The Education of an Editor

1
The
Reading Problem

Why and how a person becomes an editor are questions with so many answers that their common ground is indistinct. In my own case, being an editor could be called an inherited condition. My father was one: For a good many years, Edward Page Mitchell served as editor in chief of the New York *Sun*. That was the old morning *Sun* founded by Charles A. Dana, "the newspaperman's newspaper," not to be confused with later and lesser *Sun*s. H. L. Mencken, who never met my father, wrote of him: "Almost a god to every young journalist. I would not have swapped a word from him, in those days, for three cheers from the Twelve

Apostles. He was to me the superlative journalist of this great, heroic land."

He was also a man with literary curiosity and taste. My mother remembered his lying in bed reading *The Little Review*, which was then serializing Joyce's *Ulysses*. "This man is crazy," my father said at one point. Then, sometime later on, he said, "No, he isn't. He's a genius."

Toward the end of his life, my father wrote a book called *Memoirs of an Editor*. It was published in 1924 by Charles Scribner's Sons, and the editor was Maxwell E. Perkins. I have a letter from my father to Max, which ends up by saying, "Please let me suggest to both Mr. Bridges [editor of *Scribner's* magazine] and yourself that as to changes, curtailments, suppressions, rearrangements in manuscript, I lost many years ago any sensitiveness or pride of authorship that might originally have existed." He appears to have been an author of exemplary behavior.

At the lunch table, we debated the right title for my father's book. One of his ideas had something to do with "climbing the editorial ladder," which I disliked and said so. I was nine then when I made my first editorial contribution. Otherwise, I was not in the least precocious.

I did take to books quite early, but in a roundabout fashion. I was reluctant to learn how to read, and for this my father bore some of the responsibility. He read aloud to me, as did others in my family, and it gave me such enormous pleasure that I saw no reason to learn how to read myself. Among my readers, a cultivated aunt, who visited us for long periods and enjoyed delicate health, played the chief role. She was marvelous at it. I can recall, but only vaguely, an assortment of fairy tales, among which I preferred the bloodiest. The quieter side of my nature delighted in *The Hollow-Tree Snowed-in Book*, in various works by Albert Payson Terhune (including *Lad, a Dog*), and, above all, in *The Wind in the Willows*. That was surely the book most treasured by my quiet side; the opposite side, aroused by martial cries and the gleam of steel, found its greatest enjoyment in *Ivanhoe*. Aunt Mary and I would actually talk like Scott's characters—usually on a walk, so as not to confuse the humdrum people.

People speak of dissatisfaction with a novel because they cannot "identify" with any of the characters. The child reader-listener identifies fiercely, totally, all the way. You adopt the hero's gestures and speech and, if possible, his weapons. If the tale involves tree houses, as in Wyss's *Swiss Family Robinson* (a book I much preferred to its great

English predecessor), then you go out and build a tree house, or at least climb a tree. This active participation in literature is most satisfying.

We lived on a farm in Rhode Island after my father's retirement. We had named it Watchapey Farm, and there was more woodland in it than tilled fields. There was a cedar swamp that became strangely dark-and-white with winter snow; and there was a grove of large old pines, which one came into suddenly, a very silent place, cathedral-like. That part of Rhode Island, South County, was granite-strewn land, and the fields were marked off by dry-stone walls. In a hidden corner of our farm stood a granite boulder at least twenty feet high, with a gnarled pine inexplicably growing out of the top of it. I figured out how to scale that rock, and when I sat up there, with only the woodland sounds, I had fine and powerful feelings of command. The landscape of our farm, Watchapey, did offer many opportunities to the imagination.

I have no recollection of the process of learning to read. It must have been fast and painless: one day I was listening to a story and on the next I was reading it myself. The books were in general the standard boys' books of the time—*Treasure Island;* Kipling's *Captains Courageous;* Jules Verne, my favorite being *The Mysterious Island;* Rafael Sabatini, now remembered only for *Captain Blood*, if at all; a fine smuggling story by John Masefield called *Sard Harker;* and Richard Henry Dana's *Two Years Before the Mast.* James Fenimore Cooper and his Indians bored me, but I liked a book about Daniel Boone by Stewart Edward White.

There was a set of small books called the Rollo stories, which I must have started with in my pre-reading time and continued with afterward. The Rollo books had been popular with children several generations before mine; I still own three of them, inscribed with my father's name and the date 1859. Written by Jacob Abbott, these short novels took an improbably earnest and well-behaved boy named Rollo on a tour of Europe, during which he learned everything that was fit for him to learn. The Salem *Register* said of Jacob Abbott that in *Rollo in Paris* "he initiates us into the preparatory arrangements for crossing the Channel, takes us to Paris, and exhibits the lions in a most agreeable and truthful manner." That was unquestionably true. I was very fond of the Rollo books.

I moved on, to *The Moonstone* by Wilkie Collins, and to Sherlock Holmes. I had been given a collection of short stories by Conan Doyle, which have been entirely forgotten. I read them over and over again. A number of prizefighting stories figured in the collection—tales of the bare-knuckle days, which Conan Doyle knew a lot about. The childhood period of my reading concludes, in my mind, with my entrancement with *Pickwick Papers*. This enthusiasm I inherited from my mother: in her old age she reread the book once a year.

But before I leave these early days of my reading, mostly given to high and innocent adventure, I must record my first Dirty Book. It was *Replenishing Jessica*, by Maxwell Bodenheim, quite famous in its time for its pagan daring. It had a suitably flamboyant yellow binding, and my father kept it concealed *behind* a row of books on one of his shelves. I found it, and somehow I knew it was off limits and so I sneaked a look. But Max Bodenheim's lush prose and heavy ironies were too much for me and I soon put the book back, behind the respectable ones.

Does the desultory childhood reading I have described have any direct bearing on the preparation of an editor? Only in a general way, I suppose: It confers a benefit available to everyone—the pleasure that becomes the habit of a lifetime, a habit that it would be inconceivable to live without. Many people, thank God, catch that habit while young, and they do not all become editors, which is just as well. But it is difficult to think of an editor setting to work without a childhood of reading to support him. It will have accustomed him to making judgments about books, and it may even have given him an instinctive sense of certain rudiments of technique, such as narrative pace.

My father had died before I started my own editorial career. It began at the Loomis School, in Windsor, Connecticut, around 1928. At Loomis, I eventually rose to editorial positions on both the school paper (called *The Log*) and the literary magazine (called *The Loom*). There was one year when *The Loom* came under the faculty supervision of an Englishman named Martin Loten-Parry, recently graduated from Cambridge. He was a tall, angular, elegant young man, a good soccer player. As adviser to *The Loom*, he urged me to use paper stock of fine quality, and I am afraid that he led us into excessive elegance. When the headmaster, Nathaniel Horton Batchelder, saw the production costs for *The Loom*, he became infuriated and read me out.

But to Martin Loten-Parry I owe an inestimable debt: he introduced me to modern literature. Because of his English class, names like T. S. Eliot and D. H. Lawrence rang splendidly in my head, in a way that happens to you only when you are young and making many discoveries.

The Loomis faculty at that time was exceptional. It included a young Russian, Dmitri de Mohrenschildt, who became a good friend of mine. He was the master on the dormitory floor where I had the job of student councillor, of seeing to it that my fellow students made their beds, cleaned their rooms, and behaved in something like a respectable manner. In return for this duty, I had the privilege of joining Dmitri in his study after lights if I needed to finish my homework. We got into long talks about books, and he treated me absolutely without condescension. I don't believe I have known a more cultivated man. He was at ease in five languages, he had published a study of Proust in *The Symposium*, and he talked to me about exotic figures like Huysmans and Gurdjieff—always with balanced, humorous good sense.

When I went home to the farm at vacation time, I became semisecretly literary. I would withdraw to my room and write poems of a free-verse, Imagist kind. My mother did not disapprove and no harm came of it.

At Bowdoin College, in Maine, where I survived most of the Great Depression and also the end of prohibition, my editorial energies went into a raffish publication called *The Bowdoin Growler*. It was allegedly a humorous magazine—heavy-handed, often foolish, and, once in a while, offensively controversial. We had a hectic time—tight schedules, rushing to the printer in Boston—by and large very enjoyable. I think *The Growler* gave more pleasure to us on the staff than it did to our readers.

I had my serious activities. I had made myself into something of an expert on avant-garde "little" magazines, like *transition; Hound and Horn; Pagany;* Eliot's *Criterion;* and the early *Partisan Review*. I wrote an article for the college literary magazine (*The Quill*) called "The Pound Era and Its Close." And my most intelligent achievement during four years of college may have been a paper on Falstaff, which I still remember.

There was a climate at Bowdoin that was encouraging to an interest in books and writing. I can recall becoming stirred with excitement when A. E. Housman's *The Name and Nature of Poetry* appeared, and Herbert Hartman, professor of English, called it the most important statement on poetry in a century. But then, to my confusion, Newton Stallnecht, another brilliant teacher, whose course in aesthetics I was taking, shook his head over Housman as merely whimsical. One year I acted as assistant in Herbert Brown's lively course in the novel, and I went to a small evening writing class given by the poet and novelist Robert P. Tristram Coffin, Bowdoin's ranking literary celebrity. I don't mean to suggest, however, that college life in Brunswick, Maine, was confined to literary studies. You can drink a good deal of beer during a long, hard Maine winter. With a student body of five hundred, Bowdoin was convivial.

Robert P. Tristram Coffin thought I was a writer, and for a while I thought so too. A colorful, immensely likable man, perhaps all too fluent as a spokesman of the New England dream, Coffin encouraged me in the writing of a short novel, called *Tom Noka*. It told, very simply, about a small boy and an old Narragansett Indian who was an expert in building those dry-stone walls that divided up the Rhode Island countryside. The book wasn't at all bad, and Bob Coffin tried to persuade several publishers to take it, including Max Perkins. Quite rightly, none of them did.

I think this may be the place to take up the often expressed view that editors—book editors particularly—are frustrated writers. I might seem to be a case in point. I am quite sure, however, that I am not. After *Tom Noka*, I did some further writing; indeed, I had two short stories published, one of them in the old *Saturday Evening Post*. But it did not take me long to reach the conscious recognition that the fact that I might write something publishable did not make me a writer. I could see that a writer was somebody who could not escape being one; that he was dominated, vivified, agonized, and elated by it. It shaped his life, and I could see that it was not going to shape mine. I don't believe that not writing has caused me the least unhappiness.

The Bowdoin of my time could not compete with the class of 1825, which was the class of both Longfellow and Hawthorne, but several writers did emerge from among us. Lawrence Hall, who joined the Bowdoin English Department, was one; and Arthur Stratton, three of whose books I later edited at Scribners. In World War II, Stratton, an ambulance driver in France, was the first American to receive the Croix de Guerre; he was later wounded at Bir Hakeim, in North Africa. He served in the OSS and then, for about ten years, in the CIA, which took him to Indochina, to India, and to unlikely places like Madagascar, increasing his odd store of erudition. On the Bowdoin campus Arthur stood out: He was very tall, thin, and gangling, and he often dressed in riding clothes. The class of 1935 nervously elected him class poet, and his class poem caused consternation. Arthur became a writer who always seemed on the edge of producing something extraordinary. He didn't succeed, but underneath his surface of quirks and flourishes, he was a brave, trustworthy, gifted man.

In college I did very well in courses in literature (and miserably in German and Greek), and I won a scholarship that allowed me a year's graduate study at Columbia University. I did not work toward an advanced degree, for I felt sure that I didn't possess the scholar's temperament. I did some free-lance journalism, but here again I did not feel set in the right direction. Perhaps because of my father's distinguished career, I had no urge to become a newspaperman. And this was the time when I was coming to the conclusion that I was not made to be a writer. And so where was I, and in what way headed? To my surprise, I became a pulp-magazine editor.

2

Tarzan
and a Marine

The biggest days of the pulp-magazine business had passed when I got my job at the Frank A. Munsey Company in 1937. In those boom days, a number of writers wrote and sold a million words a year. According to legend, one pulp publisher would sniff a manuscript (to determine its age), heft it (to estimate its length), and then, if the story smelled new and had a usable weight, he would send it at once to the printer, thus avoiding the nuisance of reading it.

The story is of course apocryphal but there was a period, in the twenties and the early thirties, when pulp publishers found, to their delight, that they could sell anything. Even in my time, several managing editors each supervised as many as thirty different magazines. I worked on *Argosy*, one of the aristocrats of the pulp world, which held to respectable editorial standards. So did *Adventure*, *Detective Fiction Weekly*, *Bluebook*, *Weird Tales*, and, of course, *Black Mask*, where Hammett and Chandler started out. There was also *Amazing Stories*, the birthplace of modern science fiction; Hugo Gernsback, the editor, was a pioneer, not altogether popular with his authors, however, because he regarded paying them as an unnecessary annoyance.

The better pulp writer was by no means the cynical and dispirited hack of common misconception ever since New Grubb Street. The good ones believed in storytelling, and their belief invested their fiction with at least simple life. They wrote with energy, taking pleasure in what they did, and the pleasure was contagious. Their work differed so manifestly from the frequent efforts we received from academics, who thought that they had arrived at the requirements of pulp fiction by analysis. They felt sure they had the formulas. But their stories were dead, and went back to their authors.

At *Argosy* we published Cornell Woolrich, a gifted, uneven writer who had an uncanny knack for creating a sinister mood and whose work turned up in Whit Burnett's famous magazine *Story* as well as in the pulps; Theodore Roscoe, who once wrote a story with five successive, brilliant endings; Ernest Haycox, who lifted the Western out of the ordinary; Robert Carse, a vigorous and accurate writer about the sea, whose books, later on, I edited and whose daughter, much later on, I married; and of course, Edgar Rice Burroughs. We consistently declined the work of L. Ron Hubbard; he then went on to invent Scientology and make a fortune.

It is true that many Westerns were written by authors who had never left the Eastern seaboard and war stories by men who would not think of taking hold of a gun. But the fact still remains that a good deal of firsthand knowledge went into pulp fiction. Among the numerous writers making a living out of the French Foreign Legion as a subject, Georges Surdez had actually been a Legionnaire, and wrote very well. Borden Chase, whose stories dealt with men digging tunnels under the Hudson River, had been a sandhog; and Bob Carse must have spent, altogether, ten years at sea, eventually winding up with a chief mate's papers. In World War II, his ship was sunk off Murmansk.

Inevitably, there were occasions on *Argosy*

when editorial standards lost out to practicalities. The later work of Edgar Rice Burroughs afforded one example. In my *Argosy* time, he was approaching the end of his remarkable career, but he still received five cents a word, our highest rate. His name on the cover of the magazine did wonders. The last Tarzan novel that *Argosy* bought was so sketchily underwritten that it amounted to little more than an outline. But it had to be made into a six-part serial, and consequently several of us were delegated to fill out the story. I shared the responsibility for one installment with Ben Nelson, and we had a weekend to get it done. In my part of the narrative, Tarzan, for reasons no longer clear to me, was operating the entire time at the bottom of a large lake. How Tarzan—and I—managed is also unclear in my memory. Ben Nelson had the apes, and they were in the jungle, where they properly belonged. With frequent phone conversations during that weekend, Ben and I synchronized the whole strange business. And for each of our brand-new words, Burroughs received five cents.

Max Brand had already become a legendary figure. His real name was Frederick Faust, and he wrote a prodigious amount of surprisingly skillful, polished fiction under some twenty pen names. But the thirty million words he published mattered less to him than his poetry, which dealt with classical subjects—a long poem about Sappho, for instance, never finished. By my time on *Argosy* he had left the pulps for the more rewarding slick magazines and the movies. But he did send us a short novel, in which the central character, I remember, was a young professor of Greek. We learned afterward that he had written it solely because he had become fascinated with Greek epigrams. In any case, the story wasn't much good and I wrote a harsh report, beginning: "The old master has slipped." It was meant for editorial eyes only, but one morning I was called into the editor's office. Looking decidedly nervous, he introduced the large man sitting there, who was Max Brand. If a junior editor on *Partisan Review* had been suddenly confronted with Franz Kafka in the waiting room, his feelings would have resembled mine. Max Brand now rose; he seemed very large. "Mr. Mitchell," he said, "I have read your billet-doux—you bastard, you. And I agree with it." We then had a very pleasant time. During World War II, Max Brand, then enormously successful with the Doctor Kildare movies, somehow wangled a war correspondent's assignment from *Harper's Magazine* and *The Infantry Journal* and went to Italy, a country he greatly loved. He insisted on pressing up to the front lines, and was killed there.

The basic training of the pulps was useful, but it did not engender respect for a writer's words. We assistants on the *Argosy* staff were accustomed to receive from the editor manuscripts that had been bought and now bore his simple instruction to us—"Fix." With that sort of editorial leeway, we cut and added and altered, without thinking of consulting the author. I recall one occasion when I added two paragraphs to a short story simply in order to make it come out right at the bottom of the page. I received a note from the author congratulating me on the improvement. We kept a sharp eye out for pulp clichés, like "he husked" for "he said huskily"; and yet I do remember that a colleague filled out a column in a story set in the African jungle with the memorable line: "'A-doom, a-doom,' husked the drums."

Pulp-magazine people tended to resemble the conventional image of the newspaper reporter. That is, they were irreverent and drank a lot. They were also—in my experience, at least—intelligent, and some of them talented, people. Lunch on payday sometimes extended to the end of the afternoon, with no reprisals; and the Christmas parties, which began in the morning, required fortitude.

The knowledgeable wives used to drop in on these parties, not primarily to celebrate but to get hold of the Christmas checks before their husbands blew the money in the nearby saloons.

I seemed to thrive in this atmosphere. Continuing on *Argosy*, I also became the editor and staff of two bimonthly publications, called *Cavalier Classics* and *Big Chief Westerns*. Each of them lasted for three issues. I moonlighted as a free-lance first reader for Macmillan, receiving three or four manuscripts a week. Macmillan paid two dollars and a half for a report of three or four hundred words on a manuscript of normal length; five dollars for an inordinately long one arriving in two boxes. This constituted my editorial life until 1943, when the war stopped it.

As it turned out, the war and the U. S. Navy did not keep me out of editorial work for the duration. I was decidedly out of it, and living in a foreign world, for the months of boot camp and subsequent training. I don't think I read anything in that time, except letters. Later on, when I had been educated as a hospital corpsman and ordered to the Norfolk Navy Hospital, in Portsmouth, Virginia, my life began to shape into a routine. I was working with seriously burned patients and I got to be pretty good at it. My first wife, Helen, had joined me in Portsmouth and was driving a truck at the Norfolk Navy Yard. When I started to read again, I took up Rebecca West's *Black Lamb and Grey Falcon*, and that magnificent book remained my reading for a good part of the war.

I might have become quite a skilled corpsman if it had not been for Captain Thomas, the commanding officer of the hospital. He got it into his head that his command ought to have a newspaper, and my records disclosed certain qualifications for editing. I was ordered to get going.

My memory of that particular naval duty centers on one man, who was our feature reporter. I don't now remember how we acquired him. He was a patient in the hospital, a Marine private first class named MacBreyer, a veteran of the Guadalcanal campaign, hospitalized for a wound, malaria, combat fatigue, and for a case of syphilis that had somehow slipped by his enlistment physical. A thickset man, with a round, pale face and wide, sardonic smile, MacBreyer was by nature irrepressibly and cheerfully disrespectful, of everything. That characteristic had not caused him rapid advancement in the Marine Corps. He came from a bleak miners' town in West Virginia, where, according to him, it was usual to pass a Saturday afternoon in a saloon brawl that might spill out onto the street, slugging out the pros and cons of John L. Lewis. Only shakily literate—he did not begin in sentences with capital letters—Mac had an instinctive gift for dramatic narrative, which was my reason for assigning him to interview patients with interesting war experiences. These men were often inarticulate or too shaken up to want to talk, but MacBreyer guaranteed to bring back a story and he always did. I did not inquire into his investigative methods. He loved his work. One day I saw his stocky body hunched over a desk in concentration and I asked him what he was doing.

"I'm puttin' the blood in, Mitch," he told me.

And it proved so. To a straightforward account of combat he had added pools of blood and shreds of bodies hanging on branches in the jungle.

Eventually I received a commission, and when I appeared on the hospital compound in an officer's uniform, MacBreyer could not contain himself. He would come rigidly to attention, snap me a crisp Marine's salute, and then collapse with laughter.

The Navy sent me to Washington, or more accurately to Arlington and to the Bureau of Naval Personnel, where, for the remainder of the war, I helped to write and edit training manuals for enlisted men. This was being done in a sensible way, for the first time in Navy history. A writer-editor worked with a petty officer fresh from sea duty and equipped with practical know-how. I collaborated with a chief petty officer on a manual for first class and chief yeoman, which we finished only a few days before the war ended. Its end meant that many of the procedures the chief and I had so carefully explained became immediately obsolete. Our manual was never published.

When the Navy discharged me early in 1946, I was reluctant to return to the pulps. That experience was finished, it seemed to me. I began to look around in book publishing, with my strongest hope lying with Scribners because of my father and his book. So I applied to Maxwell Perkins for a job, and at once the procedure of job hunting became unusual and even puzzling. Max was most friendly; I even received the impression that he wanted to hire me. But there appeared to be practical difficulties that baffled him. At one point he remarked with some irritation that there wasn't any "place" for me; I felt better when I realized that he meant any place to sit. He sent me to talk to several different people in the firm, none of whom seemed to know why they were talking to me. Finally, Max arranged an appointment for me with Mr. Scribner —but with the warning that Mr. Scribner was plan-ning a trip and very busy with passports. It turned out that he was going on a Caribbean cruise, requiring no passports.

Mr. Scribner received me in his charming unassuming way. Whatever Max decided was fine with him, he said, and he hoped to find me at Scribners on his return. I reported all this to Max in his office, and he nodded, seeming pleased. I could see that he was not wearing his hearing aid that morning so it was necessary for me to shout something crucial. I shouted: "Mr. Perkins, he didn't say anything about money." Max wagged his head and said he would have to speak to Charlie about that.

The phone call finally came from Perkins, telling me that I had a job and inviting me to lunch. I arrived at this occasion in naval uniform, for during my time away, my civilian clothes had been stolen. As we walked to Cherio's, on Fifty-third Street, his favorite restaurant, Max asked me what I thought the mood of postwar writing would be. I had the sense to answer truthfully—that I didn't know. After lunch I asked him when I should start to work, expecting some free time to buy some clothes. He looked at me in surprise and said, "This afternoon." When I alluded to my Navy uniform, he said, "Well, you're not ashamed of it, are you?" I told him I was damn sick of it. In any case, I failed to make my point; he postponed my reporting for duty until the next morning, and I worked for at least a week at Scribners as a lieutenant, junior grade. In arranging my employment, Max had done a characteristically thoughtful thing. He told me that he had been hard up for money when he came out of the Army after World War I, and so now he had fixed it for me to be paid weekly for the first month. The Scribner system, he said, was payment monthly. It was somehow typical that Max had this detail wrong: Scribners paid twice a month. But in that moment none of the details mattered, for I was working for Max Perkins at Scribners.

3

Max Perkins
and the Pulp Editor

In the act of writing a book the writer is very much alone. Various people interest themselves in what he is doing—such people as wives and husbands, editors, literary agents, critics, and, now and then, a psychotherapist; but for the most part they remain quite outside the work that holds the writer absorbed. The ability to go inside, to enter into the writer's solitary enterprise without intruding, was the rare thing that Maxwell E. Perkins possessed. He used his gift modestly; he did not consider his function to be in any sense equivalent to the writer's. And yet to that writer Perkins became invaluable.

Max Perkins strongly believed that editors ought

to keep themselves anonymous. Instead, to his irritation, he became renowned during his lifetime, and he has become even more so since his death. But I think that if he were alive, Max would find some odd, logical, New England way to dismiss his fame, and so I don't feel disloyal when I try to add a little more to the public knowledge of this extraordinary man.

Maxwell Perkins worked in a small corner office on the fifth floor of Scribners. In appearance the little room was nondescript, the only distinguishing features being a portrait of an early Scribner who resembled General Grant and on the oak desk an ashtray designed in the shape of a Roughrider's hat. Perkins sat there with his manuscripts and his visitors, customarily wearing his felt hat tipped back a little on his head. You could never be sure whether or not he would be equipped with his hearing aid. If not, you needed to speak up.

Max's habit of wearing his hat in the office has been much discussed, and possible explanations can be found in A. Scott Berg's comprehensive biography *Max Perkins: Editor of Genius.* I'm not sure it matters much why he wore his hat; working with him, we accepted it without speculating. It is true, though, that the hat could be startling, even unnerving, to a visitor unprepared for it. The first time the literary agent Bernice Baumgarten came to see Max she found herself nervously apologizing. She could see that he had been about to go out, she told him, gesturing at the hat. At that, Max took off the hat, looked at it, and put it back on again.

Max frequently paced. After a spell of work he would stroll around the fifth floor, his hands clasping the lapels of his jacket or sometimes with a sheaf of manuscript still clutched in one hand. He might pause beside your desk, standing there a moment in companionable silence; or he might wander over to where Charles Dunn sat and take up the running discussion they were having of some aspect of the Civil War. Mr. Dunn* had been at Scribners forty years, serving chiefly as first reader. No first reader in American publishing has been so overqualified. He was a chess player, a violinist, an ornithologist, and sound in Latin and Greek. In his younger days he had been a sturdy hiker and—even younger—he had pitched on the Princeton baseball

* Use of proper names: Perkins, Dunn, and Wallace Meyer called each other by their last names, although they had worked together for thirty years. Perkins and Wheelock called each other "Jack" and "Max." Everybody else, including the president of the firm, called Dunn "Mr. Dunn." I called Max "Mr. Perkins." I don't recall that he called me anything.

team. He was a lovely man, a bachelor, with one secret vice, which everybody knew about: He frequently chewed tobacco while reading manuscripts.

Max Perkins had the most remarkable eyes. There was nothing judgmental in their steady look; it was calm, receptive, and curiously warming. His eyes made all the more impression because of his silences. The silences of Max Perkins had become famous in the publishing world. It was claimed by one observer that Max sat through an entire lunch with an author without once speaking. The author of course spoke a great deal, and departed after the meal looking exhilarated. John Hall Wheelock, Max's colleague, contended that a genuinely shy person would be incapable of remaining silent in the way Max did. His taciturnity seemed to be a natural and integral part of his Yankee makeup— and that Yankeeness he was proud of, I am sure, for he mentioned it often in his letters. It was extraordinary that so reserved a man could win another person's trust with seeming ease. That rare capacity was an achievement of personality, and it was probably more important in the composition of Perkins' editorial genius than his taste, his flair, or his analytical skills. The writer sitting beside Max's desk, talking, was discovering with immeasurable happiness that he had come to someone who cared about his writing precisely in the way he himself did. And later on, as the writer proceeded with his work, he felt Max's constant, reassuring presence.

In her memoir, *Too Strong for Fantasy*, Marcia Davenport said this about her editor and friend:

"Max was a foundation of my world and you do not think of a foundation as other than indestructible. I find to my amazement that he was born in the same year as my mother. It never crossed my mind that he was eighteen years older than me. Max was ageless and Max was timeless. He was the instinctive contemporary of every writer with whom he worked—and they ranged from old parties to this century's giants to brash or timid youngsters writing their autobiographical first novels through which Max discerned the talent that they had. Max was the extension of each writer's self. Yet there was never a man who was more entirely himself. He had strong views, robust prejudices, his own scrupulous code of life. But he never invoked those in judgment of his writers who were a weird lot like any assortment of writers, moved to write about worlds and more importantly, their inhabitants, amongst whom Max would have been appalled to find himself in reality."

Perkins reserved his infinite capacity for listening for his writers; that patience did not extend to the rituals of business. He flatly refused to hold formal editorial meetings. People at meetings, he explained to me, felt obliged to say something, with the result that they usually said something foolish. In office matters in general, Max quite easily became exasperated. He liked to point out that publishing was not an exact science—a contention that has never caused dispute. Displays of temperament by the staff made him impatient; we had enough of that, he said, from the authors.

Max's impatience with office procedures included vacations. He considered them inefficient and a nuisance and frequently said so in letters to his authors. In my innocence, I walked smack into this prejudice of his during my first year at Scribners. I needed a week off, which was due me; but when I asked Max, he said nothing. I waited, and he still said nothing. Finally I left his office and went to Wallace Meyer for advice. He recommended that I take my week without further discussion, which I did. It was not mentioned again, by anyone.

As John Hall Wheelock wrote, Max Perkins' ir-

ritability was part of his charm. And so was his
sense of humor, which, like other sides of him, was
quirky and surprising. Shortly after I came to
Scribners, I gave him a manuscript report in
which I scathingly dismissed the book, with all the
cleverness that young editors should learn quickly
to avoid. I remember his slight, pained smile as he
read the report, and then he pointed out that my
remarks would not help him in writing a letter of
rejection. Would I try again? Some time later he
came into the office I shared with Mr. Dunn. I was
still hard at work. "Mitchell," Max remarked to
Dunn, "is taking half an hour to refute himself."

Max Perkins' search for the new voice, for the
page of writing that comes alive, never flagged, although he was a weary man in the last years before
his death in 1947. When a piece of writing caught
his attention, he stubbornly hung onto it, sometimes in spite of incomprehension by his fellow editors. And that distressed him, for he was not arrogant in his opinions. He would shake his head in
bewilderment when others could not see the quality he saw in the work. His gift for the discovery
of literary talent has become so much the Perkins
legend that his shrewdness about commercial pros-
pects has been forgotten. But he had it. He recognized and enjoyed the storyteller, and he gave his

full editorial attention to such dissimilar writers as Arthur Train and Taylor Caldwell. On the only occasion I can remember when Max seemed even remotely boastful, he told me that he had started the modern detective story going by encouraging Willard Huntington Wright, the art critic, to become S. S. Van Dine, the creator of Philo Vance.

In choosing nonfiction, Max was fallible. His judgment suffered from his relish for odd, controversial notions. He clung determinedly, for example, to a book called *Will Shakespeare and the Dyer's Hand*, which supported a new candidate for the authorship of Shakespeare's plays. Max had a newspaperman's love for a "story," which sometimes caused him to disregard a solid piece of work for something more idiosyncratic and arresting. In the fields that interested him, however, like the Civil War, he helped to bring about some notable books. It was Perkins who urged Douglas Southall Freeman into his monumental studies of Robert E. Lee and Lee's lieutenants. Max seized at once on the idea of publishing a book of Mathew Brady photographs (to become *Mr. Lincoln's Cameraman*). And then—rather characteristically—he neglected to check details in the text. It abounded in small errors.

Max was fortunate in his two colleagues, John

Hall Wheelock and Wallace Meyer. Wheelock, Max's friend from Harvard days, brought an unusual degree of cultivation to his editorial work, as well as the sensitivity of a poet. Wallace Meyer, an exceedingly modest, retiring man, worked on a book with a scrupulous attention to detail wholly unlike Perkins' editorial style. The exacting job of seeing Douglas Southall Freeman's biographies into publication eventually came to Wallace, an assignment for which he was perfectly suited. In difficult editorial decisions he was perceptive and unshakable, a steadfast ally to have. I will not forget a very troubled conference with Mr. Scribner about the problems in *From Here to Eternity*, by James Jones. Wallace said quietly: "I think he has the finest and most shining talent to come to us since Ernest Hemingway."

For many years, Perkins had the great good fortune of Irma Wyckoff as his secretary. He invariably addressed her as Miss Wyckoff, but, in his understated New England fashion, he confided in her. He relied on her and was most demanding; she calmly put up with him and kept many matters straight, including Max's spelling.

The contradictions in Max Perkins' nature reveal themselves in his letters. The ex-newspaperman who enjoyed an upsetting notion was also a thoughtful, reflective man, with a sense of duty laid firmly down by a Puritan conscience. Again and again in his letters, Perkins alludes to Erasmus and Luther. He saw in Luther the great danger of righteous certainty. In a long letter to Thomas Wolfe in 1937, he wrote with an eloquence he was incapable of in speech:

"But I believe in democracy and not in dictators; and in government by principle and not by men; and in less government if possible, rather than more; and that power always means injustice and so should be as little concentrated as is compatible with the good of the majority; and that violence breeds more evil than it kills; and that it's better to sizzle in the frying-pan unless you're sure your jump won't take you into the fire; and that Erasmus, who begged his friend Luther not to destroy the *good* in the Church because of the bad in it, which he thought could be forced out with the spread of education, was right, though not heroic, and the heroic Luther wrong—and that Europe is the worse for his impetuosity today."

The book belongs to the author. This is a principle that every book editor will publicly subscribe to, even though some may do so with reluctance in their hearts, and may not abide by it throughout the working day. For Max Perkins, that simple principle was absolutely fundamental; it must, he believed, control the editor's every act. In actual fact, it is quite easy to forget that the book is the author's own. It isn't uncommon for a bright editor to think of a way to improve a book; but if the "improvement" distorts the writer's view or alters his tone of voice, then the editor has reached the biggest peril there is for him. As Max said in a letter, when an editor thinks he knows more about a writer's book than the writer, "he is dead, done for, and dangerous." Max Perkins had a singular gift for making editorial suggestions that were completely in the spirit of the writer's work. He advanced these suggestions tentatively, never as requirements. To the writer, they seemed to have sprung from his own imagination.

I received a small but clear lesson in respect for the writer's book soon after I came to Scribners. I was reading galley proof of a historical novel (the title of which I have forgotten) when I thought of an improvement in the opening paragraphs. It would affect only a few words. I went to Perkins and he agreed with my idea. Greatly pleased with myself, I was leaving his office to make the changes at once when he mildly remarked that of course I would need the author's approval. The former pulp editor hadn't thought of that.

I had only a year and a half as the new boy before Max Perkins' death in June of 1947. We could all see that he was worn out and unwell. Once in a while, for no apparent reason, Max would invite me to have a drink with him at the Little Bar of the old Ritz. He never said much on those pleasant times; in fact, he did not ever say very much to me during the year and a half that I worked for him. But on the morning that Wallace Meyer told me that Max had died, I broke down. I had the strange feeling that we had talked a great deal together.

4

Inheritance of a Lucky Beginner

I landed abruptly in a situation that was unnerving and yet invigorating for a young editor. The responsibility was given to me for the care of several writers with established reputations, two of whom had only recently come to Scribners and largely because of the presence of Max Perkins. Understandably, I worried; and then I decided my only possible course—not to try to be Max Perkins, and not to forget him.

One of the first writers I inherited was the black novelist Zora Neale Hurston. Every writer's reputation, if it lasts, goes through inevitable ups and downs and ins and outs, and that has been especially the case for Zora Hurston. In the twenties and the thirties, she figured importantly, and with her particular flamboyance, in the Harlem Renaissance. Zora carried on two writing careers in those days, as a novelist and as an anthropologist and folklorist whose mentor was the renowned Franz Boas, at Columbia. Digging into the folkways of her native South, and particularly into hoodoo, Zora Hurston published her findings in scholarly journals and then in a book called *Mules and Men* (1935). Several years later she brought out her second and finest novel, *Their Eyes Were Watching God*.

By the time Zora came to Scribners, in 1947, she had lived through as many tribulations as triumphs. She was unforgettable; everything she did was arresting, stimulating, and usually improvident. A figure of ample proportions, she dressed in bright colors and wore turbans. The cheerfully gaudy appearance seemed exactly right for her as soon as she began to talk, which she did at once. The vibrant force of her personality poured from her with a display of zest and wit and colorful idiom that held you fascinated. She conveyed the impression that nothing could faze her, and in fact, very little did. Our first meeting left me delighted and dazed.

Zora had started to work on her novel *Seraph on the Suwanee* (1948), which Perkins had taken at the urging of Marjorie Kinnan Rawlings. In *Seraph on the Suwanee*—to be her last novel—she did not write about blacks. Set in Florida, her home state, the book told the story of a young poor-white couple who diligently made their way in the turpentine and sawmill country on the banks of the Suwanee River. Zora wrote in an idiom usually thought of as Negro, wanting to show, as she told me, that that way of speech also belonged to the crackers. The novel centers on the young wife, named Arvay. In a letter to me, Zora said of her: "I get sick of her at times myself. Have you ever been tied in close contact with a person who had a strong sense of inferiority? I have, and it is hell. They carry it like a raw sore on the end of the index finger. You go along thinking well of them and doing what you can to make them happy and suddenly you are brought up short with an accusation of looking down on them, taking them for a fool, etc., but they mean to let you know and so on and so forth. It colors *everything*."

As the novel progressed, Zora repeatedly went off on tangents, and the editorial job was to rein her in, trim her back, from time to time, so that the book would retain some semblance of proportion. These efforts of mine Zora accepted with good humor, and steamed ahead. Finally done, *Seraph on the Suwanee* could not take a place with Zora Hurston's best work. The novel repeatedly flares and then gutters, with the author never fully in control. But the pungency of the language gives the book something all its own.

Shortly after the publication of *Seraph on the Suwanee*, when Zora Neale was living in New York—in East Harlem—she was plunged into something that shook her resilient spirit. I received a phone call from the well-known lawyer Louis Waldman, a friend of Zora's: he told me that she had been arrested for committing an immoral act with a minor and that she had no money for bail. That evening Whitney Darrow, senior vice-president of Scribners, and I went to court and then to the Women's Prison on Tenth Street, in Greenwich Village, and got Zora out. She stayed that night with my wife Helen and me in our apartment.

The charge against Zora was totally false; eventually the case was dismissed. At first, Zora coped with the mess by means of a combination of indignation and humor, but then the black press got hold of the story, and *The Afro-American*, with evident relish, gave it lurid and inaccurate treatment. That devastated Zora; she wept in my office. And not long afterward she moved away from New York, to Florida.

Down there she kept on writing, but in an increasingly slapdash way, and I had the unhappy duty of turning down two manuscripts from her. She showed not the slightest bitterness. But she was broke and scrabbling, and at one point she worked as a domestic for a wealthy family. And then, when things had become very dark, she sold an article to *The Saturday Evening Post* on Senator Taft (Zora had become a political conservative). That sale provided the money for the happiest experience of her last years. She rented a little one-room cabin in Eau Gallie, and this is what she wrote me about it, just after I had declined a novel from her:

"I am very happily located. Here in this little house I wrote *Mules and Men* years ago, and have always intended to come back here to live. So now I am back in my little house, and though facing a paved street, two blocks of trees around me on three sides. No neighbor's radios and record-players to listen to. The place was quite shaggy when I arrived a month ago, but I have the joy of clearing it and arranging things like I please. About 15 cabbage palms and five shady oaks as a background to start landscaping from. There is a flowing artesian well about fifty feet from the house, and already I have arranged a bit of ornamental water. I am planting butterfly ginger around it. My eastern limit is a low pile of stone left from an old ice-plant. Against the low line of stones I have planted pink verbena, and around the palms and the park-like ground west of the stones, I have scattered bright-colored poppies. Going to let them run wild. The Indian River, touted as the world's most beautiful river, is two blocks to the east of me, and so there is ever a good breeze. As you know, it is not really a river at all, but a long arm of the sea cut off by sand-bars, at times less than a quarter mile wide from the Atlantic. The tropical water is so loaded with phosphorus, that standing on the bridge at night, every fish, crab, shrimp, etc., glows as it moves about in the water. When the surface is disturbed, it scintillates like every brilliant jewel you can mention . . .

"Living the kind of life for which I was made, strenuous and close to the soil, I am happier than I have been for at least ten years. I am up at five o'clock and in bed around nine every night. I do hope that you and yours are experiencing something like my delirium of joy."

For five years she had the little place. But her fortunes were going down. She worked at various jobs, she wrote a biography of Herod the Great, an impossible book which we and others declined. She took those rejections gallantly. She made no complaints. It was only after her death in 1960 that I learned that the year before she had entered a welfare home, destitute. It was necessary to take up a collection in order to pay her funeral expenses.

And now Zora Hurston is having her own renaissance. At the center of it there is Robert F. Hemenway's admirable book *Zora Neale Hurston: A Literary Biography*, in which the author patiently untangles Zora's tangled life. Magazine articles about her have appeared, and her work is taught in colleges. *Their Eyes Were Watching God* has recently been reissued. Robert Hemenway makes the point that as a black individualist, a fierce defender of the separate identity of black culture, Zora Hurston anticipated the black nationalists of today. And she was, belligerently, a feminist. If she were around today, I suspect she would forsake her little house with the ornamental water to come charging back into the world again.

Josephine Herbst has not yet been rediscovered, but she stays vividly in the memory of many of us. In my own memory, she sits in my office leaning forward with a sense of eagerness, the expression of her round, almost girlish face wholly intent; and then in a quick response, she rocks back and forth with laughter, her blue eyes brilliantly alight, exclaiming in the Midwest accent that she never lost: "I can't stand it!"

You felt her warmth at once. You received all of her attention and she responded fully, with sympathy or indignation or delighted amusement. She was a woman of ideas and strong convictions, and she spoke eloquently. And she also spoke with her special distinction about the homely things that gave her pleasure, like cooking and gardening.

Josephine Herbst came to Scribners around 1940, a friend of Hemingway and already a well-known figure in the American avant-garde. Her reputation rested principally on her trilogy about an American family—*Pity Is Not Enough*, *The Executioner Waits*, and *Rope of Gold*. Because of the time and her viewpoint, those novels had caused her to be labeled with the now almost forgotten term "proletarian writer." She was, it is true, a political radical and had been drawn into the ideological ferment of the thirties; but "proletarian writer" seems a feeble, inadequate way to characterize Josie Herbst.

Her book *Satan's Sergeants* was published by Scribners during Max Perkins' lifetime, but when he died, he had not quite finished reading the manuscript of *Somewhere the Tempest Fell*, her last novel. I became, as Josie put it, "the fellow pilgrim in this book's journey." It was a complex book, perhaps too loaded down, but certainly deserving of far more attention than it got. For the central character Josie had created an immensely successful writer of mysteries, Adam Snow, who used the pen name of George Wand. His original, or at least starting point, Josie told me, was Max Brand, whom she had never met but whose career fascinated her.

My editorial role with respect to the novel consisted chiefly of worrying over the fact that only one copy of the typescript existed. Josie did not make carbons, claiming they were too much bother when one rewrote and rewrote. But while my contribution was distinctly minor, we did become good friends. My wife Helen and I visited Josie in Erwinna, her home in Bucks County, and one summer we had the use of her house for several weeks. Violent thunderstorms kept knocking out the lights and the kitchen stove just before dinner. Somewhat depressed by these results, I reported the storms to Josie. Yes, she said, weren't they magnificent?

The Erwinna house provided a center for her life. It was essential to her; although she was often away from it, she always returned. It was a small eighteenth-century stone house, whitewashed inside, built on a gentle slope, with a stream in front of it and a hayfield to one side. Somehow, poor as she was, she managed to hang onto it, and there she happily gardened, entertained her friends, and enjoyed solitude, which brought the opportunity, as she said, for "reflection."

Josie Herbst was born in Iowa. All her life she remembered the cornfields; remembered running through them as a child, through a magical green world. She came to New York right out of college and got a job on *The Smart Set*, reading manuscripts for H. L. Mencken, whom she always spoke of with affection. She sold the magazine a few stories of her own. Then, in 1921, she went off to Europe, beginning her long history of getting into the thick of things. Weimar Germany . . . the expatriate's Paris of the twenties . . . Russia . . . Cuba during a peasants' strike—she was there. She accompanied Dreiser and Dos Passos to a miners' strike in Kentucky; and in 1937 she went to Spain, up to the front lines of the Civil War while other American observers remained in the Hotel Florida. The experience in Spain had a profound effect on her, as it did on so many other idealists. Through those years of exploration, Josie supported herself as a correspondent, barely scraping by.

She was poor throughout her life. In 1948 she wrote me:

"I have been in my own little cave all summer with an awful lot started and stopped and started again. Things swarm so and out of the buzzing I have to get some order and will. What wonderful things one could write if there was an alert, welcoming, intelligent audience. I had no sooner thought that, and I often think it, when, reading Goethe, I came upon the same lament. If he could toil up his mountain without too much of an ideal audience, I ought to be able to stumble up my own little hill. I think if I knew I should have fifty dollars a month for the rest of my life I would be happy as a lark. But even so, I shall probably work it out."

I have never known anyone whose capability for friendship surpassed Josie Herbst's. In the world of writing, Hemingway, Dos Passos, Conrad Aiken, Katherine Anne Porter, William Carlos Williams, Saul Bellow, Jean Garrigue, John Cheever, Alfred Kazin, Hilton Kramer were all close friends. And there were many who had nothing at all to do with writing, like her farmer neighbor, a member of the Communist Party, who mowed her hayfield without charge.

For her friends, Josie's letters counted almost as

much as her presence. Single-spaced and often in one long paragraph, they moved in a sparkling rush, describing spring in Erwinna or eagerly and brilliantly discussing some new young writer. One must read them, she wrote me, "with the wide open enthusiastic mind willing to see the idea and the craft wherever it manifests itself." She was not lecturing me; she expected "the wide open enthusiastic mind" to belong, as a matter of course, to her friends. The knowledge that she did expect it was sustaining and strengthening for me, and I suspect for others. When I sent her an early copy of *From Here to Eternity*, she wrote:

"Sure it has flaws, quite a lot of them, but it has a spine and that is rare right now, has been rare for some time in American fiction, by and large. It is the spine I respect. The rest he can learn. You can't learn the spine. You have to have it."

Toward the end of her life, Josie got the idea for a book about writers. "In this world," she wrote me, "they are the last voice to be hushed, and I want it realized." Then, not long afterward, she had more to say about the book:

"It is about literature and life and the inseparable connection the two should have—the source of one, in the other—and the tradition that seems to me the undying and vital one and that has been obliterated

so much during the forties by all sorts of worm-
iness, by the emergence of a kind of sickness
which takes pride in its disease; not as Dostoevski,
who was always bringing in the contrast of some
bright sun that showed the sickness for what it
actually is."

That book she never finished. How greatly one
wishes that she had.

Lyrical, outraged, perceptive, and funny, Josie
Herbst's letters fully expressed her. But I have
never been able to feel that full expression to be
true of her fiction. She wrote fluently and often
with power; she made technical innovations, which
Dos Passos later used. And yet I sensed something
constraining in her work, a kind of formalism that
limited her. She went after big and difficult themes,
and surely with all the mind and feeling necessary
to a novelist. When she finished *Somewhere the
Tempest Fell*, she wrote Max Perkins in this way:

"But what I was after as an over-all picture was
the myth—the myth by which people live even
when they do not realize it. There are good and
evil myths, and some of them, like Rome, do fall.
But you know during the thirties I was preoccu-
pied with what men do about their lives, how they
struggle to find some solution, then after Spain I
had to conclude that there was something within

mankind that was deeper than what they performed. I have tried to indicate some of it here, and if I have succeeded only in being provocative about the nature of man and his fate, I shall be satisfied."

Josie Herbst died of cancer in 1969. After seven novels, her last book was *New Green Worlds*, a beautiful account of John Bartram and the early naturalists. At the memorial service for her, Alfred Kazin spoke; he told us about something Josie had said shortly before her death, which her doctor had entered on her medical chart. She had said: "I want you to give a final message to my friends. Tell them that I do not repent, that I love life unto eternity, love and life."

Zora Neale Hurston and Josephine Herbst came to Scribners—and to Max Perkins—when they were well along in their careers. He had not figured in their writing lives. But with Marcia Davenport it had been wholly different. She brought to Max the idea for her first book, a biography of Mozart; he told her without hesitation to go ahead with it. From that day in 1930 until his death seventeen years later, he helped to guide the course of Marcia Davenport's work.

It is amusing that Max should have sponsored one of the finest musical biographies of the day. He knew and cared nothing about music. The story goes that when his daughters lured him to a concert, he said at the end: "Don't clap—they might do it again." But he knew of course of Marcia's musical inheritance as the daughter of Alma Gluck. And he must have seen quite early in their relationship a quality in her that he spoke of in a letter; he said that she was "unconquerable." That was surely the strength he relied on to sustain her as she found her way through the three books, all differing, that made her reputation as a novelist— *Of Lena Geyer, The Valley of Decision,* and *East Side, West Side.*

Marcia Davenport is markedly not a dependent person. But she counted greatly on Max; to a degree, she wrote for him. When he died he was not replaceable. Wallace Meyer, whom Marcia liked and respected, followed Max as her editor; and then I succeeded him.

I scarcely knew her then; I wondered whether it would be possible for her to accept me as her editor at that point in her career, after her long association with Max Perkins. But she did accept me (graciously concealing whatever misgivings existed), and as we saw more of each other, we came to be wholly at ease. I made a few very minor suggestions, which Marcia accepted, on her short novel *The Constant Image.* Then, for a time, I thought she had no book under way, until I discovered that in fact she was circling warily around two books: a novel, only in sketchy fragments, and an autobiography. One afternoon, after lunch at her apartment, she took me into her study. She gestured at two piles of manuscript—one fiction, she said, and the other nonfiction—and asked me to pick the book she should write next. I patted the typescript that became her memoir, *Too Strong for Fantasy*.

Of course she wasn't seriously depending on my choice, and I am not guided by second sight. I think, though, that I suspected that the autobiography was her choice also. Max Perkins had wanted her to draw on autobiographical material for fiction, and her life offered a rich supply of experience. She knew of course that parts of that experience would be painfully difficult to write about. And it surely must have been so when she wrote for the first time about the death of Jan Masaryk. Just before his assassination, Marcia had gone from Prague to London, where Masaryk expected to join her. They planned to marry.

After she had finished *Too Strong for Fantasy*, Marcia told me that she had many times lost confidence, that she had even come to doubt her ability to write at all, and that my belief in her book had helped her. I had not forgotten Max's remark about her unconquerability. _Too Strong for Fantasy_ is a remarkable memoir, written with a combination of grace and strong feeling, which are distinguishing qualities of Marcia as a person.

The struggle in writing _Too Strong for Fantasy_, with the seizures of frightening doubt, happens again and again in the working life of a true writer. I think Marcia would agree that even after long practice in the craft, the act of writing with serious intention does not ever become easier.

Two young men in their twenties, recently out of the Army and World War II, began as novelists at the end of Perkins' life. Max discerned the promise in Vance Bourjaily and in James Jones; and in Bourjaily's case, Max saw his first novel to completion. I can remember my own excitement when Perkins, without comment, gave me the manuscript of _The End of My Life_ to read.

It is difficult to think of two novels about World War II more dissimilar than _From Here to Eternity_ and _The End of My Life_. The four main characters in Vance Bourjaily's book drive ambulances in the Middle East, with the sound of guns only in the distance. The novel contains scenes in a New England college and in Greenwich Village, where the writing carries an echo of Scott Fitz-gerald. But, more important, the writing has the spirit of the author—the attractive spirit that made Vance and his wife Tina such a pleasure to be with, even at those large Bourjaily parties filled with people apparently determined to terminate the Bourjailys' lease.

The End of My Life makes its headquarters in Beirut. For more than thirty years, I have kept a clear memory of one scene in that book. One of the young ambulance drivers, sitting in a street of the "forbidden" Arab quarter, learns to play the Arab pipes under the guidance of an old Arab musician while the natives gather around in delight. It is an indelible scene.

On publication, *The End of My Life* received pleasant but scarcely excited attention. Then, somewhat later, the book got a second wind from the appearance of John W. Aldridge's critical study *After the Lost Generation*. Aldridge devoted a chapter to *The End of My Life*, saying, "No book since *This Side of Paradise* has caught so well the flavor of youth in wartime, and no book since *A Farewell to Arms* has contained so complete a record of the loss of that youth in war." Aldridge's admiration carried all the more force because of the magisterial fashion with which he dismissed numerous other writers.

Vance Bourjaily's second novel, *The Hound of Earth*, came out some years later, and I was its editor. Here, Vance tackled a theme that loomed over us: the guilt for Hiroshima. The main character, a scientist from the Manhattan Project, gives up his work, his family, his identity, in an attempt to flee from his guilt, only to be captured at last. Most of the action takes place in the toy department of a large store at Christmastime, and Vance made the most of this milieu, with his particular adroitness and vivacity. On the whole, however, I don't believe the novel serves its intention with the success of *The End of My Life*. The story and its central figure do not prove adequate for the theme.

In the years immediately following Max Perkins' death, Scribners continued to look for novelists who were starting out. I had a hand in the first publication of Robert Wernick, Borden Deal, and Oscar DeLiso; in the spare, poetic, haunting tales by Sigrid de Lima (*Captain's Beach*, *The Swift Cloud*, *Carnival by the Sea*), and in John Clellon Holmes's first novel, *Go*, which recorded the Beat Generation before it had gained its name. Finding a first novel seems to me the most satisfying pleasure an editor can have. The publication, however, can be frustrating, and the final results will ordinarily put both author and publisher in a bad humor. Every year we are told that it grows harder to publish a first novel, and yet, as the gloom thickens, the first novels continue to appear. They do so because publishing of course cannot live for long without new writers, and also because every now and then a first book startlingly succeeds, like *From Here to Eternity*.

5

Eternity
and Afterward

The first I heard of James Jones was early in 1946, when Max Perkins handed me a manuscript called *They Shall Inherit the Laughter*. This was Jim's first novel, revised after correspondence with Perkins. A clumsy, ill-proportioned book, describing a soldier AWOL in his hometown during wartime and raising persistent hell, the novel nevertheless had a power that impressed us—Perkins, Wheelock, and me. But its faults looked too big to make another try at revision seem promising. Jim had said in a letter to Max that he wanted to write about life in the peacetime Army, and Max at once fastened on that, with an option of five hundred dollars. That was how *From Here to Eternity* got under way.

When Max Perkins died in the next year, I wrote Jones the sad news. Here is part of his response, dated June 30, 1947:

"Dear Mr. Mitchell,

"Your letter came today. There is not much for me to say. Some things you feel you cannot write because the words have been used too many times before and have grown old and you do not like to use those words because they are a sort of indignity to what it is you feel. Anyway I guess I do not need to say it to you. . . .

"My parents both died when I was overseas, which is probably just as well, and the relatives I do have are estranged from me over the question of whether I should go to work or write. That includes my uncle and my sister and lately my brother, who are the only ones left now. And so I have sort of had for Scribner's and for him and his faith in me the feeling a young man usually has for home. My father told me once when I was a boy in one of his less sober and more maudlin moments that any time I got in trouble if I would get to him and tell him first, before anybody else told him, he would always back me to the limit and that is sort of what I felt for Mr. Perkins somehow, and

through him for Scribner's. I had read about Tom
Wolfe and him and the feeling that was between
them and had transposed myself there in Wolfe's
place in my mind, although of course I never said
it. But I guess in life such a thing only happens
once between any two men and there is never a
repetition of it.

"It was a very hard letter you had to write me,
an awkward situation and probably not easy. I
went to Scribner's because of Mr. Perkins and
what I'd read of him in Wolfe and I think once I
even told him that but I find that now I still feel
like Scribner's is that home. I would like to know
who it is I am to work with from now on, because
I would prefer to work with one man, an individual to an individual. Rather than with a group. Of
course you did not say exactly and I do not expect
you could. But I would rather get it all straight
now. From your letter and from the time or two he
mentioned you, and since you are the one familiar
with my stuff, but mainly for the first two rather
than the last, I would like to work with you if it is
all okay there."

It was okay at Scribners. Before Max's death,
Jones had written something like two hundred
pages of *From Here to Eternity*, not all of it in final
draft or final order. As sections of the novel now

began to come in to me, I had the exhilarating experience that is an editor's highest reward: the increasing certainty that he is watching the growth of something uncommonly fine and perhaps enduring. While the novel progressed, we kept up a steady correspondence. It was only a couple of months after Perkins' death (and I was still "Mr. Mitchell") that Jim wrote in some despondency:

"I work very slowly, and painfully. Now and then I'll write like mad for a week or two and knock myself out and then it's a page or two a day until another spasm seizes me. In the over-all, it's very very very slow going. And I can't help worrying because I've never, to date, completed anything. For almost four solid years I've done nothing much but write and haven't earned a penny at it, and have not published a word, and see no immediate prospect of doing so. Truly, there seems to be no place at all in our society for the artist who is really in earnest. And all the dumbjohns always hollering about what's wrong with art in our time. All of which shows the importance of being earnest, I guess . . .

"You mustn't mind me. I seem to work by fits and starts. And this is one of the fits."

Eventually, our letters ranged in odd directions. At one point—and I have no idea why—we discussed Evil, and I recall some disagreement about it. In another letter I urged Jim to read Jane Austen. What I had in mind I can't now remember. Perhaps I was simply curious for his reaction. In any case, I did not get one, for one reason or another.

A year after Jim's despondent letter just quoted, I received another (June 1948) which took him from furious gloom into his own particular kind of comic relief:

"Nobody knows how much I want to get it done and out. I don't know why exactly but it seems like a goal and that I will be a changed person when it is. Maybe it will prove to me that I can actually write a book that is worth publishing, and that I can rest on that knowledge and relax from then on. Then, too, it's been so damned long I've been working on this. Some damn fool is always asking me about "that book" I heard you been writing for the last three years, how long does it take to write a book, anyway, when you going to get her finished, or've you given her up altogether.

"Nobody believes I'll ever finish it, and I'm damn near of the same opinion myself, any more. I just go on writing and writing, on into eternity, a long line of typed pages stretching off like railroad tracks coming together, right on to the Millennium, and beyond, on one book, the same book, the forever book, the book that never has an end, only a beginning, the eternal serial.

"I feel better now. I see I've slipped off into rhetoric, so I must be feeling better now. Whether this tells you anything or not, at least it will inform you of the great martyrdom I am suffering for my art. Rahrahrah. . . .

"You know, you're a wonderful punching bag, you know it? You don't bounce back and slap me in the nose like so many punching bags are apt to do, both the actual and the simulated. I can beat on you all day.

"Well, you write me."

Jim made several trips to New York while *Eternity* was in progress, and we got along well. We were very different, and yet about certain essential things, we thought alike. Jim possessed the gregariousness that lasted his lifetime, the ability very quickly to establish a relationship with a stranger. Once interested (and he was easily interested), he went straight at the person, asking, probing, carefully examining everything said. And people were drawn by his sometimes ferocious forthrightness and by the country humor he employed so cannily. I think that in those days the quality most marked in him was his untiring alertness. The small black

notebook he carried steadily gathered entries—
notes for the novelist, rather than promising phone
numbers, although he welcomed those as well. Jim
had a habit of winding up his description of someone he had met by saying "a very strange man"
(and it was often a dramatic understatement). We
talked about other writers, of course; he told me
once that whenever I mentioned a new writer I admired he had two instantaneous reactions—gladness
and jealousy.

In those young days, Jim was by no means an
easy man. For all the gregariousness, he was strung
tight; he could become harsh, even savage, lashing
out when something outraged or disgusted him.
What made this all the more difficult was the peculiar dogmatism with which he had been indoc-
trinated by his mentor, Lowney Handy.

Jim drank a lot and carried it well, but when
the liquor eventually took hold, his exuberance
alarmed orderly citizens. I remember a winter evening after a party at our house in Piermont when
several of us were strolling down the icy, quiet
street. Suddenly, with a happy cry, Jim hurled
himself straight forward in a sort of flat dive that
brought him chest down with a terrifying smack
on the frozen pavement. This took place directly in
front of the Catholic church. Jim got up unhurt.

Years later, with Jim an older, wiser, quieter man, the rambunctious reputation persisted. People would approach him warily, soon to be won over by the friendly and courteous man they had not expected.

Jim sent in the final section of *From Here to Eternity* with a letter dated February 27, 1950. He said: "I really feel very peculiar. Not elated. Not depressed. But peculiar. Maybe humble. So little of what I think this novel is and may be is so little due to me. I want to tack on a series of acknowledgments, at the end, later."

Two months later he wrote to Jack Wheelock: "I want to be free of this book as soon as I can. Simply because any attachment, thought on it, pride in it, any kind of hanging on to it at all, will be taking from the next one."

We at Scribners knew what we had in that four-teen-hundred-page manuscript. That required no great publishing percipience. I wrote to Jones that I believed it to be a great book—the only time, I think, that I have said those words, so commonly thrown about, to an author.

I proposed some cutting to Jim, to which he mostly agreed; but he did give me an equable warning about cutting for the sake of "propriety." In a letter of March 1950, he wrote: "You know there is nothing salacious in this book as well as I do. Therefore, what ever changes you want made along that line will be made for propriety, and propriety is a very inconstant thing."

I sent him the manuscript in sections, with the proposed cuts marked with a penciled parenthesis at beginning and end. If one could leap over the marked passage without any difficulty or loss, I argued to Jim, then the passage needn't be there. I mention this simple method of work only because it appealed to Jim, and he told me he applied it himself to later writing.

The painful, taxing job, almost submerging us in matters of propriety, came with the galley proof, after the lawyers had read it. The issue was obscenity: the fucks and shits and explicit details that could endanger a book in those dim, faraway days when Norman Mailer spelled the word "fug." We did not misspell it, but we were instructed to ration it by Horace Manges and his colleague Jack Raskin, Scribners' lawyers. They gave us an arbitrary number of four-letter words to eliminate. Day after day in the Scribner office, we struggled to get them out, an especially difficult task because Jim's ear was so exact that to change a word in dialogue would throw the line out of kilter. We kept a daily scorecard of our progress with the fucks. Jim went at it doggedly, getting to his feet from time to time to pace around in torment. He never took the easy way out, but eventually he began to treat the dreary job as a game, and I believe he even got a certain amount of fun out of it. Finally I went to Mr. Scribner* to report that we had done all we could, although we had not met the lawyers' quota. Mr. Scribner cheerfully accepted our word, which Jim always remembered with gratitude. And when *From Here to Eternity* came out, while it caused some cries of shock and outrage, only one threat of censorship arose, in the Post Office Department, and that did not develop into an action against the book.

Published in February 1951, *From Here to Eternity* had an immediately spectacular career. I remember, at the beginning, the generous statement about the book from Norman Mailer, who was struggling with *Barbary Shore,* and one from Dos Passos that was admiring but grumpy about the bad

---

* Re several Scribners: The Charles Scribner who was Max Perkins' contemporary and president when I came to work I allude to as "Mr. Scribner." His son, who ran Scribners for most of my years there, I call "Charlie Scribner." Still another, younger Charles Scribner is now hard at work in the firm, but I have quite unfairly left him out.

language. There was the phone call from *The New Yorker*, doing a Talk of the Town piece: Mr. Ross wanted to know how much the book weighed (five pounds, I think). And I remember Jim, with his sudden fame and wealth, standing with me in front of a Scribner Bookstore window filled with books by and about Scott Fitzgerald and saying that there was a lesson to keep in mind.

A year after the publication of *Eternity*, I went out to visit Jones in southern Illinois, where, just outside the town of Marshall, the "Colony" had come into being. Financed by Jim, it belonged to Lowney Handy—a place where she could bring together young writers and drill them, coax them, bully them into writing great novels. Lowney had played an undeniably important part in the beginning of James Jones's career as a writer. Just out of the Army, a lonely and mixed-up man, he had met her in his hometown of Robinson, Illinois. She supported him with her complete faith in his future. She took him into the Handy home and gave him a room; she read and debated his work with him; and—twenty years older than he—she became his mistress. Her husband, Harry Handy, a quiet, capable man but an alcoholic, appeared to accept the situation, undisturbed. He and Jim were on friendly terms.

Lowney Handy's defiant contempt for social conventions as well as her devotion to writing drew Jim to her. In truth, the force in her went far beyond dedication: It was obsession, surcharged with megalomania. Her belief in herself and in what she could accomplish with her writers had the intensity of madness. At the close of her relationship with Jim, she harassed him in her fury at his marriage.

At the Colony that summer, Lowney made me welcome. As the editor from New York, I had a place in her grandiose plans and so, with me, she became soft-voiced, humorous, and warm. She put me at ease. But the other Lowney, ruler of the Colony, could explode into screaming, strident obscenities. The colonists rarely disobeyed her. She believed that she could make a writer of anybody, and she went at it by an odd combination of hit-or-miss intuition and sheer drillwork. She set all her writers to copying published work—Hemingway, Dos Passos, Faulkner—until she felt them ready to do their own writing. There may have been some rudimentary merit in her method, as a limbering-up process. But of course it could not, and did not, accomplish what she confidently expected. Lowney had read in a wide, disorganized fashion. Dickens wrote for children, she thought; and yet she admired Arnold Bennett. Prominent and influential in her reading were some books of doubtful validity on occultism and Eastern thought (some of which, unfortunately, affected Jones's second novel, *Some Came Running*). Lowney also held strong and curious views on diet.

The Colony, on my first visit, had an impromptu look. There was a long building containing a series of tiny rooms, in which typewriters rattled. A screened-in structure served as kitchen and dining room where everyone ate, Lowney doing the cooking. There were several cabins, (one of them Lowney's), some tents, and finally, Jim's big, luxurious trailer. Brick walks ran here and there, to no apparent purpose. During the day, the scene was made to appear even more unfinished by the continual arrival of trucks dumping loads of used brick. Obtained from the oil refinery in Robinson where Harry Handy was in charge, the used brick afforded a useful chore for the colonists in off-hours. They cleared their minds by laying brick.

At least three motorcycles stood around. I was taken on a ride at high speed, which, thank God, was terminated by a sudden rainfall. Afterward, Jim wanted badly to give me motorcycle lessons, but I declined. I did not experiment with the trampoline either; but, to my astonishment, I beat him once in target shooting. Just once, however.

Marshall, Illinois, was a pleasant, tree-shaded town, a farmers' town. Saturday evening Jim took me in because they still followed the attractive, dying American custom of holding band concerts in the square. As we stood there in the crowd, two teen-age boys came up and greeted Jim by his first name. One of them had a question about *From Here to Eternity*, which he asked seriously and without embarrassment. Jim answered him with equal seriousness, in a way characteristic of him all his life.

Jim Jones's second novel was a huge book, *Some Came Running*, a story set in a Midwestern town very like his birthplace, Robinson. During 1956, the year he finished the novel, I heard from him frequently, and I think that a half dozen selections from his letters give a glimpse of the shifting, divergent moods of a writer pouring all his energy into his work.

February 16

"I am now ten pages into Chapter 43; a total of just over three hundred pages that you have not seen. (I counted up) I would expect to have the five hundred by the end of next month, unless something unforeseen happens. This will carry it up to the summer of 1948, and one more chapter (※44) will end book three the craft. I think you'll be real pleased with it. Lowney and I are. There's a total of around 1240 pages now. I figure I ought to be able to wind everything up in no more than 9000̸ more. (God, I wrote nine thousand!) 900 more. Maybe I can do it in some less.

"Maybe we should sell it in a boxed six volume set, like Churchill's Memoirs, hunh?"

July 23

"The pressure on me is getting terrific; almost more than I can stomach. Its much worse than the ending up of Eternity, which I just sort of breezed through. Most of it is due to the fact that I know everybody is alerted to the end of this one, and know that all the barbs and hooks and knives and harpoons with which literary people love to score each other are being sharpened up no doubt. There is no remedy for it, I guess, except to plug away my five to six hours every day and try to forget it the rest of the time."

August 19

"Did you know that I now have a parakeet?

Won him at the county fair for thirty cents—and then had to spend fifty dollars buying equipment and feed for him. He would, of course, turn out to be a neurotic one. All he does is walk up and down his perch with his hands behind his back and frown nervously. Thats the most expensive thirty cents I ever spent. You don't know a good bird psychiatrist, do you?"

September 12

"And if I ever find out that you did in fact lie to me about what you thought about revision, even in order to help me along as you thought at the time, I'll be through the book [*sic*] as far as you and I are concerned."

September 28

"I've just finished proofing it this morning, and by God Im even kind of awed by it myself! I don't honestly, in my secret heart, believe that Im that smart; or that good."

December 16 (*Running* has been finished)

"I'm starting on this fast; so I will have the phones and doorbells all off for a week or ten days. Nor do I even intend to even go out of the house during that time, so I won't be able to go uptown and get the mail . . . I want to spend a week entirely alone, just reading some and thinking."

The manuscript of *Some Came Running* was not only vastly outsized, it also contained, according to the long-suffering lawyers, an array of obscenity problems. The morning Jim and I started to work in the Scribners library, the job seemed truly overwhelming. Several people at Scribners had clearly intimated to me that they disliked the novel, which did not increase my fortitude. I looked at the great pile of manuscript and said to Jim that we would have to chew away at it, bit by bit, day by day. He nodded gloomily and said he trusted me.

We cut, but not enough. Jim would not give up certain irritating mannerisms, like the many and repeated adverbs. When the novel came out, the reviewers—already poised for the attack after the success of *From Here to Eternity*, as Jim had foreseen—lambasted *Some Came Running*. There were only a few supportive voices, like that of Robert Kirsch. I have recently had occasion to reread *Some Came Running* with particular care, and I'm convinced that in spite of its verbosity, its ineffective stylistic experiments, its dubious "philosophizing," this novel, which so resembles Dreiser in its faults, can match Dreiser in what it accomplishes. It is a book that has been greatly maligned. Willie Morris has written that "no one has written about middle-class America—what later would be called 'middle America'—with the discernment and, moreover, with the *love* that he brought to *Some Came Running*."

I don't think that Jim Jones ever did have the full support of the reviewers after *Eternity*. Their inclination was to leap on his weaknesses, or to invent them, and sometimes they seemed to enjoy doing it. But from other novelists Jim received respect, and lasting affection when they came to know him well. His three closest friends were William Styron, Irwin Shaw, and Willie Morris. Many of the writers who admired him were of a wholly different cast from his own; but they recognized, writer after writer, the power of Jones's conviction about their art.

While Jim was still engaged in writing *Some Came Running*, I paid another visit to Marshall. By then he had built a house on the outskirts of the Colony. This expensive and impractical structure, planned by Jim and engineered by Harry Handy, contained a magnificent stone fireplace, a large playroom, glamorous bathroom appliances, but only one bedroom. Poking around, one found everywhere the accumulations of Jim the collector: knives (a lifelong hobby), Southwest Indian jewelry, hats, katchina dolls, chess sets, expensive

books on ballet. Willie Morris has said of Jim in
later life that "one was struck by his sensitivity
to finely crafted things." That was always true of
him. At the time of my Marshall visit, he had
taken up woodworking and was making himself a
workbench. He went at it meticulously, having
first indulged himself in some expensive power
tools. The bench claimed so much time, according
to Lowney, that she was going to send it to
Scribners to fulfill his contract. Finally the bench
was finished, and splendid, and I don't believe Jim
lifted a hammer again.

A column by J. Donald Adams in the *Times
Book Review* implying that *Some Came Running*
had been written solely to make money infuriated
Jim, but otherwise he took the beating from the
critics without rancor. I am sure, however, that the
harsh reception of the book provided the impulse
to write *The Pistol*. It began as an idea for a short
story, and then he set out quite deliberately to
write a short book and to write it in exemplary
prose. When he gave me the finished manuscript,
he urged me to look carefully for any error in the
use of language. I do not remember finding any.
With that good small book, *The Pistol*, Jim made
his only response to his critics.

Jim Jones had been a lonely child and, when not

writing, a restless, driven man. Then, in 1958, he had enormous good luck. He met Gloria Mosolino; he fell immediately in love with her, and almost as immediately they married. It was a remarkable marriage—remarkable in the simple fact of its total, permanent success. Virtually from the day of their meeting, Gloria became indispensable to him. The marriage did not alter the fundamental shape of Jim's nature, but it is certain that his abiding happiness put him at a new ease with the world.

Later in 1958, Jim and Gloria Jones moved to Paris, where they lived for fifteen years. There Jim wrote *The Thin Red Line*, the combat novel that the protagonist of *Some Came Running* was writing when he died. It can be argued that this book was Jones's finest single achievement, exact and complete in carrying out his intention, and the only American novel of combat that can stand with *The Red Badge of Courage*. When Jim returned to the U.S. in 1961 to deliver the manuscript, there was very little editorial work needed. It consisted of reducing the excessively detailed descriptions of terrain, and Jim did this in the Scribner office.

With four novels published, one of them a legendary best seller, James Jones was now an established, prominent, successful writer. That made him, in the competitive business of book publishing, an object of intense interest. Several publishers approached him with offers that he turned down, and finally Dell-Delacorte made one that he felt he could not decline. His letter to me from Paris began: "This is probably the hardest letter I will ever have to write." At Scribners we had no choice but to release him from the contract for the novel that became *Go to the Widow-Maker.*

The day the *Times* ran a story about James Jones's changing publishers, a telegram arrived at the office, addressed to me and to my colleague Donald Hutter. (I was addressed as Burroughs "Banal" Mitchell.) The message rejoiced in Scribners' loss of Jones and predicted that the firm would soon sink into oblivion. The telegram was signed by two writers whose novels Don Hutter and I had recently declined. I suppose that by now, after more than fifteen years, I should have forgotten that act of childish malice, but I have not. I have, however, forgotten the names of the two writers. The bleakness of that day at the office was relieved by a gracious act. George Schieffelin, the executive vice-president of Scribners, stopped me in the hall to commiserate with me over the loss of Jones. In a casual fashion, he went on to say that he hoped it might cheer me somewhat to know that he and Charlie had raised my salary.

Jim Jones left Scribners in 1965, and in the next years I saw little of him. Both of us had some feeling of strain, I suppose, which gradually wore off. Besides that, he and Gloria were living abroad, with their children, Kaylie and Jamie. Occasionally Jim and I would correspond, and I recall a surprising phone call from Paris one New Year's Eve, wishing me a Happy New Year. Then, after fifteen years in Paris, they came home in 1973, eventually to settle down in a farmhouse on the eastern tip of Long Island. Jim loved it there.

Jim was writing *Whistle*, the third novel in his war trilogy. He knew he was seriously ill, weakened after several bouts of congestive heart failure, and he was exhausting himself, writing twelve and fourteen hours a day, in order to finish his book. The last days and hours in the hospital, while he struggled to dictate the final actions in his novel, have been most movingly described by Willie Morris in *James Jones: A Friendship*.

Ross Claiborne, at Delacorte, asked me to edit the manuscript of *Whistle*. While Willie Morris, working from Jim's taped notes, skillfully prepared a summary of the last two and a half chapters, I went over the manuscript, catching the small things

I knew Jim would have caught in a final reading and making only those minor changes that I felt certain he would have accepted. He had not quite finished his big book, but he had done substantially what he wanted to do. *Whistle* fully and powerfully existed. When it joined *From Here to Eternity* and *The Thin Red Line*, Jones had given us a revelation of the effect of war on men that is unique in American literature.

The dark view of human probabilities that James Jones expressed in his fiction may seem out of accord with his personal life in the adult years—a vigorously enjoyed life, filled with family happiness and many friendships. But that apparent contradiction has occurred before in literary history. It is possible that a man holding the dark view will try exceptionally hard to make the most of every good thing he can find in his lifetime.

Jim Jones's friend Tom Chamales began his writing career as a sort of outpatient at the Handy Colony. He did not live there, but nearby, and he did his first writing under Lowney's supervision. Nobody's supervision, however, remained in force for long over Tom Chamales.

He was a Greek-American from Chicago. His father was well situated there; an owner of nightclubs and other enterprises, and he had enjoyed the respect of Al Capone. In World War II, Tom Chamales served in the OSS, fighting for a year and a half in the Burma campaign, behind Japanese lines. The Kachin people gave him the title of Duakaba, or high leader.

Tom drew on the Burma experience for his first novel, *Never So Few*, published in 1957. A graphic book, it derived its special quality from Tom's knowledge of and affection for the remarkable Kachins. He wrote a second novel, *Go Naked in the World*, also autobiographical but not nearly so interesting. He had advantages for a writer in his abundant energy, his intelligence, and the unusual scope of his experience. But he was in a great hurry for fame and I don't believe he had in him the capacity for the long accomplishment. There was to be no test of that, however: Tom died in a fire in Los Angeles in 1960. He was thirty-six.

In the late fifties, around the time of Jim Jones's marriage (where Tom was best man), Chamales and Jones were frequent companions in New York. They made a formidable pair. A big, powerfully built man, Tom moved with catlike grace and spoke in a soft voice. He had charm and manners (and incidentally, like Jim, he got on beautifully with my then ten-year-old son, Bruce); but, unlike

Jones, he had an unpredictable and dangerous streak of violence in him. The two of them used to drop in on me often at Scribners. Filled with martinis and picturesque tales of each other's adventures, they would hover around my desk, never sitting down, Jim growling away in what Gloria has called his "cowboy's voice" and Chamales laughing softly in an unnerving fashion. At length, they would take off, having told each other that I had work to do; but they might then visit Harry Brague, my fellow editor and old friend. Harry coped with these occasions with calm amusement.

I think that in Jim Jones, Chamales saw everything that he wanted to be. But what he failed to perceive was the steadfastness. Or perhaps he did see it, but found it unattainable.

6

Not Slick

*A*mong the first people I got to know in the publishing world in 1946 was one of the most exceptional men in it. He was Diarmuid Russell, the literary agent, and we were close friends for almost thirty years, until his death in 1974. His literary agency, Russell and Volkening, came into existence largely at the instigation of Max Perkins, for Max had introduced Russell to Henry Volkening, who had been a friend of Thomas Wolfe when they both taught English at New York University.

There is a familiar and unkind image of the agent—literary, movie, or theatrical—which represents him as a thoroughly slick character who employs two phones at once and tells lies over both of them. This is not fair, although some traces of the truth may exist in the caricature. Literary agents have taken a firm place in literary history because of associations like those of Elizabeth Otis with John Steinbeck and Harold Ober with Scott Fitzgerald. And now, as the business ramifications of the written word have become increasingly complicated, involving a variety of rights and bringing a few writers enormous sums for their books, the power and function of the literary agent have expanded. Without a robust temperament, an agent won't survive in his nerve-wracking occupation, the pressures of which may lead to gross exaggeration, evasiveness, and the double cross.

These hazards did not affect Diarmuid Russell; his nature made them inconceivable. He and the conventional image of the agent seemed a world apart. It could not be said that Diarmuid employed either a hard or soft sell. He simply spoke his mind. When he went so far as to call a new client "a lively writer," you knew that he had made a discovery of some consequence. He not only had the gift of literary good judgment but he also had the resolution to support it, and he took on writing that other agents might consider hopelessly unsalable. Quite often his literary taste proved, in the long run, to be commercially sound. In business negotiations, one soon discovered that behind Diarmuid's calm, reasonable manner there lay a final inflexibility. With his partner, Henry Volkening, he built up a remarkable agency, numbering among its clients Bernard Malamud, Eudora Welty, Saul Bellow, Barbara Tuchman, and Vance Bourjaily.

Diarmuid was born in Ireland, the son of A.E., the poet, painter, agriculturist, mystic, and leading figure in the Irish Renaissance. A story Diarmuid told me about his father seems to me to exemplify the sometimes bewildering integrity of son as well as father. A group of Irish writers once approached George Russell with the offer of the editorship of a new Irish magazine. They had got together the money and they proposed a substantial salary to A.E. He refused at once. The salary was much too large, he said; much more than warranted. The backers retired and reconsidered, and only after they had managed to lower the salary to an amount that A.E. considered suitable did he accept the editorship.

One of Diarmuid's gifted and most illusive clients was the short-story writer Maeve Brennan, also born in Ireland. For more than twenty years her short stories had appeared in *The New Yorker*, but her work was not brought together in a book until *In and Out of Never-Never Land*, published by Scribners in 1969. And that publication was accomplished with curious difficulty. Maeve Brennan is the only writer I have encountered who ap-

peared genuinely reluctant to bring out a book. I
have no idea why she held back, but I doubt
whether that collection of twenty-two stories
would have ever come out without the support I
received from Howard Moss and other friends of
Maeve. The book contained three stories about
Rose and Hubert Derdon, and three more appeared
in her second book, *Christmas Eve* —a marvelous sequence of stories about a tender courtship and a
marriage that increasingly isolates husband from
wife. While I worked on the two books of
Maeve's, I received various notes from her, more
often than not decorated with a drawing of a
round, smiling face. The face expressed a reassur-
ingly friendly spirit in the author. But in dealing
with Maeve's reluctance I had baffled moments,
and on one occasion, I remember, I consulted Diarmuid for guidance. After all, he should be able to
tell me how to proceed, I pointed out, his being
Irish himself.

Diarmuid said, "I don't think I understand the
Irish."

Slickness is a very loose but still useful word,
which has a particular, semiliterary application. In
the days when magazines flourished by publishing a
lot of fiction, the big national weeklies and month-

lies—*The Saturday Evening Post, Collier's, American, Good Housekeeping*—were called in the trade "the slicks." The term came to have a double meaning; it described the glossy coated paper on which the magazines were printed, and it also defined the stories published. They were slick fiction—smoothly written, adroitly manipulated toward an agreeable resolution. The pulp-magazine tale, unpretentious and straightforward, embodied more honest storytelling than the deft fiction in the slicks.

The term "slick" will always remain convenient, for the writing it identifies will never disappear. While it is essentially lazy writing, because it avoids the difficulties of honesty, the writers work very hard to achieve the necessary facility. In novels, slickness appears especially in "genre" fiction—that is, in historical romances, gothics, science fiction, and mystery novels. To write in one of these categories without resorting to slickness requires on the writer's part the constant exercise of integrity, as Dorothy Salisbury Davis has shown in her crime novels. Throughout the thirty years she has been publishing, she has been resolute in not allowing herself to take slick evasions. The unidentifiable Newgate Callendar of the *Times Book Review* once said of Dorothy Davis that "her special strength lies in transcending the puzzle, using it as a vehicle to develop character." The requirements of the circumscribed form of the mystery novel make it especially difficult to deal with character without superficiality or fakery. Dorothy Davis has succeeded. In this, she is not of course entirely alone; one thinks at once of the English detective-story writer P. D. James. But the achievement remains a rare one.

My association with Dorothy Davis began in 1948 and became the longest continuous editorial alliance I've had. Max Perkins used to say, somewhat mysteriously, that one's friends never wrote good books but that did not preclude the possibility of a writer's becoming a friend. Dorothy Davis did become one, and, in fact, the friendship may have sometimes made her distressed and uncomfortable when she wanted to speak out with a quite legitimate author's complaint. I can remember occasions, however, when she managed to overcome the reluctance.

She is a bright-faced woman, with the air of being on the alert for good news. Certainly she delights in giving it. Underneath her liveliness there is solid rock of determination; she possesses that valuable writer's quality of staying power, which Balzac may have had in mind when he said that "constant toil is the law of art." The capacity to persevere is one shared by such radically dissimilar individuals as James Jones, C. P. Snow, and Dorothy Salisbury Davis.

Perhaps I ought to explain at this point that while at Scribners, I dealt with a good deal of the crime fiction, never a large list. Other editors became involved; Harry Brague, for one, and Elinor Parker, who is as expert on the mystery novel as she is in her specialty of books on the crafts. I did find that my pulp-magazine training proved helpful: I had learned which conventions of plot and narrative had become entirely worn out. As a mystery editor, I lacked the desirable ingenuity that relishes plotting and so I was inclined to judge a book by its plausibility and tension, by the interest of the characters and of the milieu. I looked for some of the qualities of any good novel.

They are to be found in all of Dorothy Davis's books. She has always pushed her achievement beyond the basic requirements of the mystery novel. She has written more than a dozen, among which, *A Gentle Murderer*, first published in 1951 and later in at least four reprint editions, has come to be regarded as a classic. Indeed, Dorothy may be weary by now of laudatory references to that one book, but the inescapable fact is that the book deserves them.

In Dorothy's early novels, the only editorial problem arose from the precautions she took to avoid the obvious. She tended to give the resolution of her plot in a manner so subtle and elided that it baffled not only me but her husband Harry as well. We managed to prevail on her to explain to simpler minds, like ours. There was a small but irritating mess, not of Dorothy's making, involving her second book, *The Clay Hand*. The copy editor extracted all the Irishness from the Irish dialogue, with the result that I had to put it back in. Dorothy Davis is herself Irish-American, which directed her interest to the subject matter of her historical novel, *Men of No Property*. That fine and neglected book told of the Irish coming to New York City in the 1840s.

I have spoken of the value of a writer's durability. It always carries with it, I'm certain, the strength to recognize and survive failure. To pursue the wrong idea, only to realize what has happened, must be the most shattering experience a writer can have. He faces the truth that the book he has been writing is not the book he imagined. It is a moment in a writer's life that requires the greatest courage. Long after she had become well established as a writer, Dorothy Davis went to work on a novel that seemed promising to those of us who knew something about it. She kept at it for perhaps a year, and then she came to that moment when she realized that what she was writing could not ever satisfy her. In a solitary decision, she burned the manuscript. She told me afterward.

This sort of lonely encounter with the truth reminds me of an experience Josephine Herbst told me about. She had promised a publisher a book of her observations on South America, and then, eventually, she came to recognize that she could not write it. After weeks of worry and frustration, she went out to her vegetable garden one morning and said to herself (perhaps aloud): "All right. You are incapable of writing that book. You have failed. And that's that." The acknowledgment of failure, she said, brought her an immediate and enormous sense of relief.

My friendship with Dorothy Davis assuredly does not afford an example, but it is true that by allowing a professional relationship to grow into a friendship, an editor makes himself vulnerable to troubling experience—to outrage and disillusionment and sometimes to great sadness. I think now, in my own experience, of the sudden death of

Sue Kaufman in 1977, which was so especially sad-
dening because her life and her work seemed to be
bringing her so much.

It isn't surprising, I suppose, that the prose style
of a writer should accord with her person. It did,
certainly, in Sue Kauman's case: She possessed the
grace, the unshowy elegance of her writing. Her
gentleness was as genuine a part of her as her gift
for shrewd, unromantic observation of the world
around her. In her fiction, her perceptions could ir-
radiate a small happening. She could give the
reader a pleasure almost like that to be had from
her great admiration, Jane Austen.

I was Sue Kaufman's editor for her first book,
The Happy Summer Days (1959), a deft, fresh
comedy of manners about a holiday on Fire Island,
and for her following novel, *Green Holly*. Then
she went on to four more books, which included
her best-known work, *Diary of a Mad Housewife;*
but we were not any longer professionally involved. We frequently did not see each other from
one year to the next. And yet the friendship stayed
firm, I always felt; and I believe that she felt so,
too. It may be that whenever an author and an editor have survived the publication of a first novel
without emotional disaster, something indestructible remains.

7

Special Information

In my thirty years as a book editor, the three "big books" I could be said to be responsible for, the commercial blockbusters, came out within five years of one another, in the 1950s. This is a little dismaying. At the time these novels appeared, my education as an editor was certainly not very far along. But also, what happened *after* the three books? Did I fall asleep? I prefer to think that I did not, and that the explanation for the peculiar concentration of best sellers into that short time lies in impersonal factors, such as publishing conditions, and luck.

From Here to Eternity was, of course, the first of the three books. The second was a novel called *Not As a Stranger*, written by Morton Thompson and published in 1954. The book has now been almost forgotten, but its nature and history are interesting. For one thing, the prodigious success of *Not As a Stranger* to a great degree derived from the "special information" embodied in the novel.

The editors of the old *Saturday Evening Post* used the term "special information" to describe the specific raw material of a story. We tend to speak of the style and the subject matter (or content) of a novel as if they were disparate when, in fact, they do not neatly separate. Neither one can exist by itself, without the other. But on the most utilitarian level a distinction can be made about subject matter in certain novels. To take two great ones, you might give a rudimentary idea of *Bleak House* by saying that Dickens deals with the workings and the evils of the English legal system a century ago; but there would be no equivalent way to identify the subject matter of *Great Expectations*. There is a kind of writer who stands at the furthest distance from special information—who, as Robert Graves says, seems to "expect the ritual of writing to produce the subject."

Morton Thompson had the most marketable variety of special information, which is medicine. His novel tells the story of the making of a doctor, a young man devoted to his calling with ruthless dedication. That dedication, dramatized in the rather cold drive of the narrative, laid a hold on the reader. But what fascinated him even more was the multitude of exact details about a doctor's life with which Morton Thompson substantiated his story: medical school, the daily office routine of patients, emergency calls in the night, crises in the operating room. All of this Thompson rendered graphically and with authority. A doctor whom we asked to vet the book before publication found the medical data unexceptionable.

Morton Thompson had written an earlier book founded in medicine, *The Cry and the Covenant*, a biographical novel about Semmelweis, the discoverer of puerperal fever. But he had become dissatisfied with the publisher of that book (as he would, ultimately, with any publisher), and he was shopping around when he came to Scribners. Thompson examined publishers with the aid of a formidable ally—his wife, who, as Francis Pindyck, had been a leading literary agent. They came to visit me together.

Thompson was a square, heavy-set man, soft-voiced, with a smile that came easily; and he had a quick wit, which, I learned later on, could turn vicious. His enormous ego did not make itself immediately visible. At our first meeting, it was his wife, Fran, who laid down the ground rules. I was to read *The Cry and the Covenant* and write my absolutely honest opinion of it. If my opinion proved acceptable, Scribners would be offered Thompson's new novel about a young doctor, a book not yet written or even outlined. There would of course be financial requirements.

The Cry and the Covenant impressed me, and Charlie Scribner agreed that we should take a chance on the unwritten novel. During its writing, I saw a good deal of the Thompsons without ever gaining a clear idea of how he came by his knowledge of medicine. He was not a doctor. He had served as a medic in the Army, he told me, and had taken part in operations. He was slightly mysterious about it all. After his death the mystery grew more ominous, for we discovered that a technical passage in *Not As a Stranger* closely resembled a paragraph in the memoirs of a well-known doctor.

A very strange man, as Jim Jones might have said, and a man accomplished in diverse ways. He could fly a plane, he did cabinet woodwork and antique restoration of a professional caliber in his shop, and he was a celebrated cook. In his first book—bearing the unforgettable title *Joe, the Wounded Tennis Player*—he presented the most elaborate recipe on record for cooking a turkey. When Fran entered a preserve of some sort in a local Grange competition, Mort entered a concoction of his own and won the blue ribbon. It was a small but somehow disagreeable competitive act.

He needed to excel, and he could not be wrong. Charlie Scribner, who has an exceedingly thorough education in the classics, found a Greek word misused in *Not As a Stranger* and gently mentioned it to Thompson. Mort flushed; he remained civil, but obviously unconvinced. A week or so later, I received a note from him saying that he had consulted a Greek scholar at Yale and that his use of the debated word was correct in a particular dialect of ancient Greece. We did not believe him, but we let the word stand. The affair had been educational.

I don't believe that anything he did appeased Thompson's restless ambition. It was ironic that he could not enjoy the satisfaction of his most considerable achievement. He died shortly before the publication of *Not As a Stranger*. Two weeks later, Fran shot herself to death.

Any editor of fiction will sometimes find himself on suddenly intimate terms with a form of special information for which he is unprepared, but I have never been confronted with anything so recondite —for me, at least—as the subject matter of Paul E.

Erdman's first manuscript. The book was *The Billion-Dollar Sure Thing* (1973), and the subject matter international finance in its most complex manifestations.

We had heard about Erdman and his book from Ray Vicker, *The Wall Street Journal* senior man in Europe, who had interviewed Erdman in a Swiss jail. He had landed in the jail as a result of the collapse of the bank he had founded in Basel. Writing a novel constituted a wholly new activity for Paul Erdman, but he had been previously published—a treatise in economics, written in German. Eventually the Swiss released Erdman on bail and he moved to England, where he finished his novel and where I first met this brilliant man.

Erdman's descriptions of the intricate workings of the international money market did not require editorial vetting; it was evident that he knew precisely what he was talking about. I did, however, make some suggestions; in particular I urged him to invent, for relief, an episode unrelated to high finance. He responded with enthusiasm, producing a scene in Paris that can be described as the Sex Scene of the novel. What is more, he gave credit where he felt credit was due, and on a national television show he revealed that Burroughs Mitchell had told him to put sex into his book.

When the Swiss put Paul Erdman in jail, they caused him to discover an aptitude that had nothing to do with international finance. It is the aptitude for storytelling. Without that native gift, his subject matter would have proved intractable in fiction. He also brings to his writing a sense of humor that alternates between the sardonic and the raffish. I suspect that Paul, as a novelist, may be one of a kind, a sport. It seems unlikely that a monetary expert and a storyteller will again converge.

The historical novelist subsists, of course, on special information. Tales of the past, like *Ivanhoe*, had given me delight as a child, and they had figured in my duties as a pulp-magazine editor. But only when I began to edit books did I become aware of the complications lying in the term "historical novel."

It is a term regarded as reductive and derogatory by a number of serious novelists who write about the past. They are quite likely to point out how inadequate the label seems when applied to *War and Peace*. My friend Jay Williams, the author of several fine novels about medieval times (*Tomorrow's Fire*), in fact gave up writing about the period that fascinated him simply because he abominated the inevitable categorizing of "historical novel."

The trouble arises at least partly from the fact that there exists a vast quantity of junk fiction called "historical." The old term "costume romance" better suits these books, in which the authors accentuate the exotic, remote nature of their material, applying to the story a sort of historical cosmetic. The true novelists do the opposite. They decrease the time distance between the reader and the period of the story. They don't think of the life they write about as "historical," for they live in it themselves. These writers have assimilated and distilled the raw materials of fact and infused them with the qualities of their imaginations. They combine in themselves the scholar and the artist.

One of the finest of these whom I've known is the British writer Hope Muntz. Her marvelous book *The Golden Warrior* came out in 1946—a novel about William the Conqueror, which in her telling reaches epic grandeur. Hope Muntz gave ten years to that book, exploring the historical material with a scrupulousness usually reserved for scholarly monographs, and in the process teaching herself medieval Latin.

On trips to London for Scribners, I usually had dinner with Hope, a friendly, direct woman who brings up William so casually in conversation that it requires an effort to realize that she is speaking of

William of Normandy, not of some relative of hers. In our talks—during which I mostly listened—I don't believe that I acquired very much in the way of historical fact. It was too complex, and she assumed too much knowledge on my part. But I did gain something more important—a glimpsed sense of the past that, by her very casualness, she made to spring to life. That sense, that glimpse, can sometimes be conveyed with more immediate, startling effect in conversation than by means of a book. And it may act as a helpful corrective by placing certain present-day matters in their proper, unimportant locations.

I have had a similar experience in conversation with a young writer whose first novel was, in fact, the last manuscript I was at all involved with at Scribners. Published thirty years after *The Golden Warrior*, this novel—*The Mists of Manitoo*, by Lois Swann—deals with Colonial Massachusetts. In writing about the Indians, the Massachuseuck tribe, Lois Swann accomplishes something extraordinary by creating their forest world in terms that are glowingly idyllic and yet firm with realistic detail. In fact, the research for that detail caused a linguistic feat that conceivably surpasses Hope Muntz's; Lois Swann taught herself the Narragansett Indian dialect. When Lois talks about the time and place she has taken possession of—New England in the eighteenth century—she passionately expresses the belief that past and present conjoin.

In nonfiction, the duties of a general editor take him into territories where he cannot possibly be knowledgeable. He can of course go to experts, but he reaches an inevitable point where he must accept the authority of the author. One of the most important books I have been associated with, *Feeling and Form*, by Susanne Langer, published in 1953, was not wholly foreign ground for me because of my excursion into aesthetics at college. But with *Feeling and Form*, I had in my hands the manuscript of a large-scale and original theoretical work, nothing less than a comprehensive philosophy of art. Susanne Langer finds that the various arts lead to a central conclusion, that art creates forms symbolic of human feeling. What makes the book of concern to everyone in the arts as well as to professional philosophers is her conviction that a theory of art must start out from the experience of the artist rather than from the postulations of the abstract thinker. And so, as she inquires into what happens when a work of art comes into being, she looks first to the creator: the painter, the poet, the composer, the novelist, the dancer. Mrs. Langer is herself a musician, a cellist, which gives her a kind of understanding that supplements her capacity for rigorous abstract thought.

I went through my editorial responsibilities with Susanne Langer in a state of awed pleasure. The pleasure, for one thing, issued from the fact that she writes extremely well. *Feeling and Form* is a difficult book, but nothing in the writing, no jargon or ponderousness, increases the difficulty. I was so impressed by the book that I think it may have been valuable in my education to discover that Susanne Langer was not unassailable. We had progressed to page proof, which fortunately was being gone over by Don Allen, a cultivated man, when it became evident that the quotations from classical English poetry weren't quite right. Checking, we found them all to be just a shade off. When I spoke about this to Mrs. Langer, she smiled and said it was possible, she had quoted them all from memory. I lost none of my regard for *Feeling and Form*, but I did acquire what is probably a healthy suspicion of the inviolability of the intellectual.

8

Silence and Cunning

The satisfactions of giving advice are considerable, as everyone knows, and advice is part of an editor's business. He gets paid to give it. This might make for a happy occupation if it were not for hidden dangers. The big one, I think, consists of inattention. Listening must precede advising, and intelligent listening I believe to be a trained skill, requiring conscious, hard effort. I have come close to editorial disaster because of not listening carefully.

The occasion I have in mind concerned the third of those novels that I have called commercial blockbusters. I was having lunch with Gerald Green, a tall, articulate, funny man charged with vigor in spite of the migraine headaches that plagued him. He had already begun his busy career of writing books, first in a collaboration with Larry

Klingman on a nonfiction account of a South Seas adventurer, a book called *His Majesty O'Keefe*. Green and Klingman had been colleagues at International News Service, where they produced vast quantities of copy every day and still had the energy left over to think up a book and then write it. Jerry Green followed that one with a novel that grew out of his lifelong fascination with anthropology; it was a historical novel—quite a long one —about the Incas in ancient Peru, *The Sword and the Sun*.

The day of our luncheon, those two books constituted Gerald Green's experience as an author. He had meanwhile moved from the wire service to television, where he became the first producer of the "Today" show. In that position he had to deal with a chimpanzee named J. Fred Muggs, an arrogant and unpleasant animal who bit Jerry. In spite of these distracting responsibilities, Green had fastened on an idea for a novel, which he outlined to me during lunch. The story was to center on an elderly doctor practicing in Brooklyn, an irascible and uncompromising man, who grew corn in the backyard of his city dwelling. Jerry proposed to combine the doctor's story, somehow, with that of a television producer who was fighting to preserve his job and who was unfaithful to his wife. All of

this Jerry described with his customary vivacity,
but thinking back now, I'm quite sure that I did not
listen intelligently. I received a confused impression: The idea for the novel sounded complicated
and unfocused, unclear in its point. I must not have
asked the necessary questions. But I did manage,
thank God, not actually to disparage the story Jerry
Green had laid out for me, and he went ahead to
write it, _The Last Angry Man_, published in 1956. In
my own defense I can say that I could not have
foreseen the powerful presence of Green's father in
the book. By his personality and his medical career,
Samuel Greenberg, M.D., invigorated _The Last
Angry Man_. And Jerry Green brought to the writing a storytelling gusto and a gift for sardonic social
observation that I had not expected. He had come a
long way from ancient Peru.

Some years later, I encountered another challenge to attention, and this time I responded ade-
quately. It was a conversation with Elliott Arnold—
again at lunch. An experienced writer, who had
published his first novel at the age of nineteen, Arnold had on his record such successes as _Blood
Brother_, but I knew his work only by reputation.
He had now got hold of a dramatic and poignant
event from World War II as the subject matter for
fiction—the feat of the Danish Underground, in

1943, in smuggling virtually all the eight thousand Danish Jews to Sweden and safety. It was accomplished within two weeks. As Elliott described the Danish story, so tightly circumscribed as to time and place, he did so with a precision and dramatic emphasis that made the possibilities of the novel manifest. It may be that Elliott's experience with story conferences in movies and television has sharpened his skill at telling a story. In any case, I did not hesitate over that one, which became *A Night of Watching*.

The juxtaposition of Green and Arnold reminds me that, among novelists, the writers who respond most equably to editorial suggestions seem to be those with newspaper training.

There has been no writer within my experience who could propose a book with the hypnotic persuasiveness of Bernard Wolfe. When I listened to Bernie, I did not have to make an effort of attention; what I had to do, I learned, was to prevent myself from being swept along in the current of his eloquence. Talking about a book-to-be, he comes close to the creative act itself as he formulates the book without hesitations, without corrective second thoughts, pausing only to draw on his cigar. I did learn to be wary when he wound up a brilliant summary by saying that the novel would be a short one. To be fair, he has written shortish novels, but it must be recognized that when Bernie writes, one thing tends to lead to another.

He accepted a substantial amount of cutting in his remarkable novel about the death of Trotsky, *The Great Prince Died*. That was one of the three books of his that we published at Scribners, but before then, around 1950, he had established his style in *Limbo* and *The Late Risers*. He wrote highly charged prose, marked with a flair for the grotesque. A precursor, Bernie Wolfe has not yet received his due credit.

A writer of nonfiction—a biographer, for example—is much more likely than a novelist to be guided by advice in the material he chooses to write about—but not at the outset of his career. I am sure that W. A. Swanberg discovered his first subject, the gaudy but almost vanished Civil War figure Dan Sickles, entirely on his own. I can remember a portion of that manuscript coming into Scribners in 1955—an interesting account of a man I had never heard of by a writer equally unfamiliar. I learned eventually that W. A. Swanberg, like myself, had been a pulp-magazine editor before World War II (his specialty was true-crime magazines) and that his hobby of studying the Civil War had led him to General Dan Sickles.

Bill Swanberg is a man holding strong moral convictions, but these are fortunately accompanied by a taste for flamboyant and even rascally individuals. Jim Fisk was certainly one, and William Randolph Hearst would also fit, in his oversized way. Among the nine books Swanberg published during the twenty years I served as his editor—one of them winning the Pulitzer Prize (*Luce and His Empire*) and another the National Book Award (*Citizen Hearst*)—the latter became the most widely known.

The idea that he should write it came, I believe, from his literary agent, Patricia Myrer, in whom Swanberg rightly places great confidence. At first, Bill regarded the prospect of a life of Hearst with reluctance. It would require a way of working new to him, for heretofore his research had been carried out in the library and now it would be necessary for him to interview people. He is a shy man, who never makes a public appearance, and he is somewhat hard of hearing. I suspect that he did not look forward to going to work with a tape recorder. He was also troubled by the fact that so much had been written about Hearst.

The concern about interviewing soon disappeared. His absolute trustworthiness became so apparent that people had no hesitation in confiding in him and his tape recorder. As he investigated his subject, his enthusiasm began to gain. When he wrote me after a trip to the West Coast in 1959, during which he talked with a number of Hearst people, it was evident that *Citizen Hearst* had taken hold. Here are portions of that letter.

"His working newspapermen regarded him with a strange mixture of nervousness and admiration. They worried about his foibles but were won over by his unfailing fairness and kindliness in dealing with them, and will defend him with a chip on their shoulder. Hearst cheerfully spent thousands on men who were sick, sending them to specialists in other cities, sending them abroad for their health, paying their mortgages, etc., doing all this with real personal concern for them. Tough and autocratic in some ways, he was enormously sentimental, so much so that he would even forgive chiselers and embezzlers if they had once done good work for him.

"He was nuts about animals, even mice. San Simeon was overrun with them. He wouldn't allow snap-traps—only the non-injurious cage type. The butler was instructed to leave choice tidbits around so the mice wouldn't go hungry. It was his first duty every morning to carry out the traps and release the mice unharmed. Hearst allowed the killing of rattlesnakes and rats. But he was in a rage when a squirrel got its leg broken in a rat trap—sent all the way to San Luis Obispo for a vet to set the squirrel's leg.

"Although he lived unwillingly in sin for 34 years, he was the most conventional of men. He preached against liquor (especially women in bars), attacked Bertrand Russell for defending adultery, and blasted Mae West for smutty movies. Some of his best editors were drinkers. One of them, from Boston, was a real souse. Hearst took a liking to him, had him at San Simeon several times for weeks, trying to rehabilitate him, but the man died of drink anyway. Hearst said, 'For a non-drinker, liquor has cost me a fortune. . . .'

"He worked all night, and often would throw his SF or LA newspaper office into an uproar with some strange request at midnight. At different times he asked for a street car bell (no one knows why), four trivets, petits fours, a dozen spring chickens with no pinfeathers, franks and buns for a children's party, rhubarb and soda, and once for $10,000 in crisp new bills. These requests, always made politely, came at times when stores were closed. Reporters would go flying around the city, arousing storekeepers and getting them to open up.

Although Hearst never said so, it was felt that there'd be hell to pay if he didn't get what he wanted in a hurry. . . .

"He has never been presented as a human being. My talks with people who knew him have made me feel close to knowing him myself and should enable me to write about him with some sympathy and rapport despite his obvious failings.

"The definitive biog of Hearst will have to be done some years hence by someone who can afford to hire a dozen or more rescarchers; the job is that big. But I'm enthusiastic about it now, and my book, within its limits, could be a good one if I can only handle it."

He handled it magnificently. He dug in, working ten hours a day and with undiminished zeal. In April of 1960, he wrote me: "I'm non-impartially enthusiastic about it because Hearst, for all his short-comings, was always doing something indefensible, inexplicable or praiseworthy, and I don't think there will be many long, dull stretches." Toward the end of that year, Bill Swanberg finished his manuscript of seven hundred and fifty pages. Apologizing for the length, he said in his own defense: "Yet I return to my theme that this fellow lived for 88 years, every one of them at a fast pace, and stuck his nose into everything."

The exasperating footnote to the history of *Citizen Hearst* is the fact that the judges for the Pulitzer Prize made it their unanimous choice, only to be overruled by the trustees of Columbia University, presumably because of the moral unworthiness of the subject.

Two of Swanberg's books grew from suggestions by us at Scribners, and one of them caused him misery. We proposed Theodore Dreiser. After some reading on the subject, Bill sounded wary. But I considered it to be the usual first symptom, the same wariness with which he had approached Hearst. I felt certain that he would find adequate rewards in the subject. I could not have been more wrong. In a letter of December 1962, Swanberg said:

"Sinclair Lewis was immature and often annoying, but he was also very funny at times. Dreiser was immature and annoying, but weird and often objectionable—seldom funny. The problem will be to maintain at least an objective if not a sympathetic point of view."

There is a clear note of discomfort in this, which I discounted. And, uncomfortable as he may have been, Bill knew that he was working with important material, and it was not in his nature to give up. Five months later he reported:

"I'm working ten hours a day but will do well to finish by Christmas. I very much fear that despite careful selection and ruthless excision of semi-important incidents, this will be a *long* book—don't see how it can be otherwise. T.D. was always riding off in all directions, juggling a dozen enterprises in addition to his women. He wrote, wrote, wrote —millions of words in letters to women alone, and by hand . . .

"I think Dreiser will emerge as one of the weirdest of geniuses, a man of fantastic energy, great courage and unique abilities, along with shocking ignorance in some areas and a complete failure to recognize his own limitations."

There was one discovery Swanberg made that affected him with something like revulsion for Dreiser. He found out that Dreiser had frequently sold to magazines, under his own name, various pieces of writing by his women friends and then pocketed the payments—all this at a time when Dreiser was financially well off. That was too much for Bill Swanberg. By a notable exercise of will, he managed to control his dislike of Dreiser and to produce a valuable biography. But here was a case, I'm convinced, where we made a bad match between writer and subject.

Our suggestion of Norman Thomas as a subject

proved a happy one. The son of an old-time socialist, Bill Swanberg could recall distributing socialist literature around St. Paul, Minnesota, as a boy. In Norman Thomas he had—for the first time—a man to write about whom he wholly admired and also liked. One could not fail to admire Joseph Pulitzer, about whom Swanberg wrote one of his best books, but it was difficult to feel any liking for him. Dan Sickles was engaging, but not quite admirable. But the fine and attractive personality of Norman Thomas sustained Bill as he plowed through the vast collection of Thomas papers in the New York Public Library and followed the labyrinthine windings of the American Socialist Party.

A dogged and meticulous researcher, greatly aided in this task by his wife Dorothy, Bill Swanberg organizes masses of material into clear and lively narrative. His books often run long, which has always worried him, as his letters show. But he is a narrative biographer and he needs room for the accumulation of detail to enhance the story. Over the years, I have watched Bill Swanberg make his way, cautiously, toward an understanding, a coherent view, of his subject. Once he finds it, he cannot be deflected.

9

The Realists

When I made my first trip to London for Scribners in 1954, I was given the authority to acquire a book on my solitary judgment. This heady responsibility may be educational, but it causes feelings of alarm when you find yourself on foreign ground with no colleagues to lean on. My assignment had been lightened in one respect; I had been told that if I came back home with no books, I would probably save the firm a good deal of money.

Quite early in that London trip, the literary agent Spencer Curtis Brown handed me an advance copy of a novel called *The New Men* and told me that the American rights were available. The author was C. P. Snow, and I had not read a word by him. But *The New Men* took hold of me; I cabled New York to find out how the several Snow novels already published in the U.S. had sold. The response to my cable was wholly depressing. What was more, I had to face the vexing fact that *The New Men* belonged in a series, by no means finished. At length, however, I took a very long breath and made an offer for Snow's novel, which was accepted. A little later on, we met at the Savile Club, and I recall that for some reason I brought up Gide's remark that while writing he did not read novels for fear of influences. In his customary way, Charles Snow thought for a moment and then said it was probably wisest, under the circumstances, to read in a foreign language. This is all I remember of the meeting at the Savile Club, but it began a friendship.

Charles Snow makes strong friendships. An outgoing man, warm and generous in spirit, he does not in the least resemble the archetypal British civil servant operating in the corridors of power. Snow is a large man with a rather stately tread, but the majestic impression vanishes as soon as you have heard a burst of his engaging laugh. He can be very direct. His civil service duties, especially during the war, required him to evaluate people with speed and precision. And underneath that professional training there lies keen native curiosity—about people, customs, occupations. The scope of Snow's inter-

ests now takes in baseball. The year the Mets won
their great World Series victory, bringing all New
York to its feet, Charles was here, this time without
his wife Pamela. It became impossible to extract
him from his hotel room when the Series was on
view. After the climax, Susan Richman, the publicity director at Scribners, who is often inspired,
purchased a regulation baseball and presented it to
Charles. He was delighted, and practiced throwing
curves into the cushion of his hotel couch.

Snow says that he knew before he was twenty
that he wanted to write novels. But he was a poor
boy; he needed the stability of a professional career,
which—with his brilliant academic record—science
offered him. And so his remarkable career begins
with a fellowship in physics at Christ's College,
Cambridge; then leads him into public life as a civil
servant in the Ministry of Labour during World
War II; to Civil Service Commissioner and eventually to a title; and still later to an important position
in Harold Wilson's government. He also becomes
what he deprecatingly calls "a pundit," and from
this activity comes the now famous essay, "The
Two Cultures and the Scientific Revolution." (It is
worth noting that at least two of Snow's titles have
fixed themselves in the language—"the two cultures"
and "corridors of power.") Throughout these busy

years, Snow kept hold of his chief objective—to write novels.

Novels spring from a variety of sources, sometimes small and unexpected ones: the personality of someone the writer has met by chance, or the flavor of a place, or the implications suddenly evident in a happening; from the writer's urge to reveal, to destroy, to celebrate, to record, to make something. It isn't always that a writer can precisely identify the starting point, the moment the book began in his head. But C. P. Snow has given a fascinating account of the conception of the Strangers and Brothers series:

"I had the idea out of the blue—in what seemed like a single moment—in Marseilles on 1 January, 1935. I was walking down the Cannebière. It was a bitterly cold night, well below the freezing point. I was staying in Marseilles for the night, having flown down from London, and was off on a boat to Sicily the next day. I was extremely miserable. Everything, personal and creative, seemed to be going wrong. Suddenly I saw, or felt, or experienced, or whatever you like to call it, both the outline of the entire Strangers and Brothers sequence and its inner organization, that is, the response or dialectic between Lewis Eliot as observer and as the focus of direct experience. As soon as this happened, I felt extraordinarily happy. I got the whole conception, I think, so far as that means anything, in a few minutes."

The eleven novels in the Strangers and Brothers sequence form a massive achievement. Inevitably, within the achievement there are soft places, and just as inevitably, the reputation of the work has fluctuated. In the long run, the fluctuations won't matter. The eleven novels will remain a permanent part of British fiction, not only because of their scope or of the mastery with which the many lives have been wound together, but most of all because of an animating force everywhere present: Snow's pressing, fascinated search into human motives.

Right now, the realistic novel gives way to other modes in fiction, but that is not to say that the realistic tradition has therefore given out. We used to hear, again and again, that the novel itself was dead. That gloomy cry has been muted by the facts—by the number of good novels by serious and innovative writers. As for the realistic tradition, I cannot believe that a current in literature so illuminating of life is likely to run permanently dry. In the tradition created by Tolstoy and Balzac and Henry James, C. P. Snow's novels, I am convinced, will hold a lasting place.

Snow's prose style has been the subject of complaint, having been called flat, or pedestrian, or dull. These charges seem to me the result of careless reading. In Snow at his best, the deceptively plain style carries a strong undercurrent of feeling. William Cooper in his essay on Snow has pointed out how subtly Snow calculates his use of language; how he varies the easy, conversational flow with the interpolation of a startlingly uncommon word or figure of speech. It is flexible, agile prose, possessing the capability of wit. It is not quite as "simple and direct" (to steal Jacques Barzun's title) as it looks.

For thirty-five years, Charles Snow steadily followed the plan he had conceived that evening in Marseilles, without losing sight of where he was headed or losing control of the means of getting there. One wonders how he managed to do it.

He writes rather slowly. Four hours of work, his customary stint, produces a thousand words in a longhand, sometimes intelligible only to his wife Pamela. He repeatedly revises. I believe that his huge accomplishment of written work can be at least partly explained by two attributes that Snow possesses to an exceptional degree—the powers of concentration and of memory.

His method of public speaking exemplifies the remarkable memory. For years when Snow lectured, he used no written text. The Godkin Lectures at Harvard require a written text, for later publication, but Snow did not refer to it when he delivered "Science and Government." That printed text runs to nearly fifty pages.

I had a fine opportunity to see Charles Snow make use of his power of concentration. The Snows were in the U.S. and *Corridors of Power* had just reached the stage of galley proof when we received urgent word from London that Harold Macmillan, then retired as Prime Minister and Snow's British publisher, had found a technical error in Parliamentary procedure in the novel. To correct it would require a number of adjustments in the plot—about a dozen of them, as I recall. They needed to be made quickly.

Charles and Pamela came to spend the night at our house in Rockland County. Promptly at nine the next morning, the three of us sat down to work —Charles with the galleys and Pamela at the typewriter so that she could copy the longer revisions. The shorter ones I would put on a duplicate set of proofs, having made sure that I understood them. From nine o'clock until two-thirty, Charles did not leave his chair; he paused from his work only to sip a glass of water. (Pamela and I had a drink and a sandwich.) As he sat there studying the galleys,

Charles appeared to be enjoying himself, to be deriving genuine pleasure from the necessity for concentrated thought. It occurred to me that the scientist was solving the novelist's problems. At two-thirty that afternoon, when he had completed the rather complicated chain of alterations, Charles had a drink.

In his association with Scribners, Charles Snow has always been alert, practical, and appreciative. When *The New Men* came out in 1955, his literary reputation had just begun to cross the Atlantic, to gain him attention. In March of that year he wrote me:

"Many thanks for Trilling's article; but the valuable thing is that he has to write about me at all. For the first time he and what I may loosely call established "aesthetic moral" opinion have to admit that a rogue elephant is on the scene. And the admission is going to have excellent effects for me on both sides of the Atlantic.

"What I confess puzzles me is that Trilling and others seem so hopelessly at sea with art which is lucid and simple on the surface, and more [word unclear] and complex as you go further down. Have they never heard of Stendhal? Who, by the way, has touched me more profoundly than Trollope?"

And two months later he said: "The American reception has meant a lot to me. I'm just at the stage when a writer, if he's going to be any real good, needs to get a second wind. With any real luck my next five years ought to be the best."

And his luck was good; the next years brought him critical recognition, honors, and commercial success. I learned about the principal honor in a characteristic letter from Snow, dated 7 January, 1957.

"*The Conscience of the Rich* has been a bit delayed, by a somewhat peculiar reason . . .

"The peculiar reason is that I was given a Knighthood in the New Years Honours List (v. *Homecoming*, N.Y. edition, 1963, Chap. 17, p. 112). For all literary purposes, of course, I continue as C. P. Snow; and I expect that in the U.S. you can disregard it completely.

"My emotions are somewhat mixed, as you can imagine. On the one side my arrogance and old-fashioned radicalism are not pleased: on the other, it would be artificial to turn it down—and I'm vain enough to chuckle at the thought that no other novelist of standing has ever gone so far in affairs (the award was in theory at least given for official work)."

We hurriedly sent off congratulatory cables.

The commercial success arrived more slowly, to his occasional irritation.

"For God's sake don't think I was grumbling. You have done a wonderful job for me, and I am basically well content. About once in every six months my wrongs well up in me and I suddenly feel outraged that I have not, in my whole literary life, had one single piece of the big commercial luck. But it doesn't matter all that much. If I had to choose between my position and Jim Cozzens', I should elect for my own. Though you might very naturally find the choice a little harder to make." (*By Love Possessed* had been published, with huge success, the year before. A strong admirer of Cozzens' work, Snow thought somewhat less of this novel.)

Early in October of the next year, 1959, I was able to cable Charles Snow that a piece of the big commercial luck was now his. The Book-of-the-Month Club had chosen his new novel, *The Affair*. In answer, Charles wrote me one of the most delightful letters I can remember.

"I heard your news last Thursday night in picturesque circumstances. I was being entertained in Leicester by a group of my old schoolmates, none of whom I had seen for 37 years and most of whom are now modestly successful businessmen. They were extremely and touchingly cordial. I became, I regret to say, distinctly drunk. Then about 11:30 in the Grand Hotel Leicester the public address system said—so the soberer members of the party said—that I was wanted on the telephone. I staggered off and heard Pam, just back from the Brain Trust and herself a little affected by whisky, reading out your cable. Gradually I got the drift of it. Then I returned to my ex-schoolmates. It was a fine evening."

The facts of his life have made Charles Snow a worldly man. But the worldliness has expanded rather than diminished a quality of his that has rare value. It is what Jerome Thale has called his "undulled capacity for wonder."

About other writers—particularly young writers —he has always been generous. He came out early and strong for Kingsley Amis's *Lucky Jim* and for John Brain's *Room at the Top*. On one occasion, while I was on a London trip, I stumbled on a discovery before he had the opportunity to direct me to it. I told him that I had found only one book, a first novel called *The Animal Game*, by Frank Tuohy. Charles said at once, in his cheering fashion, that I had taken the only new novel in London worth talking about.

The American edition of my discovery, *The*

Animal Game, did not make a fortune for its author and Scribners. But it introduced an accomplished realist who, particularly in his short stories, writes with unerring precision, with a combination of humor and pathos that you do not forget. Frank Tuohy has led a nomadic existence, living (and usually teaching) in Brazil, Poland, Greece, Japan, and the United States. He brings to bear the same, exact gift for social observation whether his setting is São Paulo or England in the thirties.

Pamela Hansford Johnson—Lady Snow—is, like her husband, a realist. C. P. Snow's fiction possesses humor as well as wit—one thinks of the Dickensian landlady in *Homecoming* and of Mr. March in *The Conscience of the Rich* patrolling his London mansion every evening to tend the clocks—but Pamela Hansford Johnson has written three novels that are outright comedies. And yet I think these books can be said to be as "realistic" in intention as they are entertaining.

The Unspeakable Skipton, Night and Silence Who Is Here?, and *Cork Street, Next to the Hatters* compose a trilogy, held together by the awesome presence of the poet Dorothy Merlin. The middle story, *Night and Silence Who Is Here?* takes place

in the United States, at a New England college;
and it contains one of the finest comic notions in
modern fiction. Pamela Hansford Johnson presents
a feverishly earnest young scholar named Ruddock who is determined to prove that Emily Dickinson was a lush. In this scholarly effort, he sup-
ports his arguments by quoting Emily Dickinson,
line after line, and when you read the lines from
Ruddock's special viewpoint, they do seem to bear
him out. As a matter of fact, I was told that the
Ruddock contention received some serious consid-
eration in scholarly circles after *Night and Silence
Who Is Here?* came out in 1963.

I cannot leave the subject of *Night and Silence
Who Is Here?* without speaking of my own contribution to the book. Pamela wanted a lively, idio-
matic American expression to describe someone
falling downstairs. I suggested "ass over teakettle,"
which pleased her and which she accepted. Since
then, however, her husband, Charles Snow, has
insisted that not one of the many Americans they
consulted had ever heard the expression. I cannot
explain this, but I remain quietly proud of my contribution.

My wife Jean once asked Pamela Snow whether
she actually laughed when she hit on one of her

comic inventions. Of course she did, Pamela said, if the author doesn't laugh, who is going to?

The arguable link between comedy and realism takes me to the black writer Kristin Hunter, whose editor I was for ten years, beginning with her first novel, *God Bless the Child* (1964). I suspect that Kristin might insist that even the outrageous individuals in her second book, *The Landlord*, were true to life. She tells there the story of the misadventures of a wealthy young white man named Elgar Enders, neurotic, but filled with goodwill toward his fellowman, especially the black man. He decides to buy and to manage decently an apartment house inhabited by blacks. Elgar wants his tenants to love him; they want to take him for all they can—which they do. The activities of Enders and his tenants enable Kristin Hunter to upset many well-established clichés about blacks and whites and their view of each other. She is up to something quite serious in the novel, making use of comedy instead of polemics.

So much sprouts from Kristin Hunter's imagination that she sometimes fills her books too full. I have the memory of her looking thoughtful—not yet acquiescent—when I've suggested a trimming back or toning down. She would think about it, and then, ultimately, she would be likely to agree.

But an editor at his worst could not succeed in depressing Kristin's comic spirit. And she also laughs aloud, she says, when she hits on a notion that pleases her.

10

Six Poets

In publishing, editorial decisions about poetry—when they are made at all—generally fall to specialists, to men and women who are themselves poets or critics. Harry Ford, responsible for Atheneum's list, represents an outstanding exception; by and large it is the specialists who make the choices for publication. That held true for years at Scribners while John Hall Wheelock, a distinguished poet himself, supervised the poetry list. He was especially proud of the annual volume *Poets of Today*, in which young American poets received their first book publication. That volume began the careers of twenty-four poets, among them James Dickey, Louis Simpson, and May Swenson. When Jack Wheelock retired, *Poets of Today* ceased publication, but the firm continued to bring out a small poetry list each year, and I had charge of it.

My qualifications did not go beyond the fact that I had read a good deal of poetry, old and new, and liked the new as well as the old. I had only the most cursory knowledge of prosody. I was an amateur, and I remained one. That is, I never raised a question about a technical weakness or urged the alteration of a line. But I was necessarily obliged to cope with the main problem, that of selecting which work should be recommended for publication. These decisions were made all the more difficult by the fact that a surprising amount of interesting new work came steadily in. I became aware that I stood in danger of sliding into a state of hopeless indecision, a paralysis brought on by my sense of responsibility to Literature. Clearly I had better not worry about Literature. What I must do, I decided, was to allow myself to be guided by the quality of the voice in the poem. If that voice—the fusion of statement and style—caused me to read the poem again, then at least I knew I was dealing with the real thing.

In actual fact, one of my chief services to the Scribner poetry list took place well before I had any editorial authority over it. It involved Wheelock's first *Poets of Today* volume, in 1954, in which one of the three collections by new poets was *Another Animal*, by May Swenson. I'm especially proud of having had a hand in its publication.

At that time my wife and son and I lived in the village of Piermont, on the Hudson River, and just a short distance away, in a little house with a garden on the river's edge, lived a remarkable woman of letters named Elizabeth Shepley Sergeant, biographer of her friends Willa Cather and Robert Frost. One Sunday afternoon Elizabeth invited me over to hear a young poet read. The poet proved to be May Swenson; the reading took place in the river garden while small boats swept past. Years later, May wrote in an inscription: "For Burroughs Mitchell, who listened in a garden long ago to a trembling poet." I don't recall any trembling; May seemed then, as always, quietly self-possessed. I do most certainly recall the effect made by the poems, read against the distant whine of outboard motors. The next morning at the office I told Jack Wheelock about May Swenson.

She is of Swedish and Mormon descent, an unassuming woman who goes her way with a determination not immediately apparent. She does not belong to any one school or group in the arcane divisions of contemporary poetry. One time when we were all talking about poets, I used Robert Lowell's handy classification of cooked poets and raw poets. May smiled and said that some vegetables were better cooked and others better raw.

She has written "sound poems" and "shape poems," and the latter became for a time her special province because she made the design so effectively express the poem's intention. Among her early poems, *Stony Beach* is a poem of both sound and shape. It may be, in fact, one of those poems she read aloud on Sunday afternoon in Elizabeth Sergeant's garden by the Hudson. Here is *Stony Beach;* you will hear the sounds of the sea in it, and see the tide sliding further and further up the beach:

The sea like
Demosthene's mouth
champs upon these stones
whose many stumblings make
him suave
The argument molded
monotonously by all his lips
in a parliament of overlappings
is vocal but incomprehensible
because never finished

Listen listen there is nothing to learn
from the sea
Listen he is lucid in sound only
convinces with broken phrases that
wizardly
the waves round out a rune over riddling
stones

Beginning again and again with a great A
a garbled alphabet he lisps and groans
and the insistent eloquence of echoes
has no omega

The artifice of the shape poems reached its most complicated expression in May Swenson's volume *Iconographs*. We had to use an outsize page for the book, for obviously you cannot carry over a shape poem from one page to the next. Nor can you depart very far from the poem as produced on the typewritten page. All this required an unusual degree of patience and care from the production department, but there was eventual reward in the fact that *Iconographs* won a prize in book design. And we had accomplished what May sought for: "To cause an instant object-to-eye encounter with each poem even before it is read word-after-word."

The shape poems obliged May Swenson to concern herself with the design of her books, but I have found that as a general rule, poets feel even more strongly about the appearance of their books than other writers do. The poems of Howard Moss, for instance, do not present any unusual difficulties to the printer. But Howard watches attentively over the making of a book of his. And of course he is right to, for a typeface or a jacket design might easily clash with the lyric beauty and the wit of his poems. That sort of discord becomes possible much more often in a book of poems than in a biography or even a novel. To make the book design wholly expressive of the poetry may be difficult, perhaps impossible, but to avoid an outright clash requires only care and taste.

Robert Creeley made the author's point in a particularly apt and succinct fashion when he wrote me in 1971 about his *A Day Book*. He said:

"I *hate* having to insist that the writing *does* have a particular character of some specific interest, but I can't for the life of me see why else Scribners chooses to publish it. That assumed, the setting becomes crucial and I won't and can't, in fact, accept any setting that isn't a factual response to the mode and nature of what's being said."

Several of Bob Creeley's books presented problems to the production department. *Pieces* required a bold typographical effect and continuity from one "piece" to the next. And *Presences*, which Creeley did with and for Marisol, seemed to spend an endless time in production. Bob accepted this with amused resignation, his usual comment being a favorite one of his: "Ah well." He is an intense, gracious, responsive man. Characteristic of him is a letter beginning, "I'm *very* happy to have your sense of the book—it really does feel like a 'new day.'"

In trying to define style in prose, George Orwell and Herbert Read have both said that it comes down to a matter of personal sincerity. If you transfer their definition from prose to poetry, it seems to me to apply very well to Robert Creeley's work. The effort for complete and exactly expressed sincerity gives the intensity to his pared-down, taut poems, with their highly personal use of colloquial language. In a *Paris Review* interview some years ago, Creeley had something interesting to say about the impulse behind his poems:

"I have been given to write about that which has the most intimate presence for me, and I've always felt very, very edgy those few times I have tried to gain a larger view. I've never felt right. I am given as a man to work with what is most intimate to me —these senses of relationship among people. I think, for myself at least, that the world is most evident and most intense in those relationships."

In 1965, Paul Engle, who was then running the Iowa Writers Workshop, sent in a collection of poems by Henri Coulette called *The War of the Secret Agents*. For some reason—perhaps because so much good work lay at hand—my resolve to act decisively did not work in the case of this manuscript. I knew (as other people did) that Coulette's poetry was better than good, that it was remarkable, and yet I brooded and procrastinated. All the while, in South Pasadena, California, Henri Coulette admirably kept his temper and his silence, although he did admit, afterward, to some agitation. I finally brought myself to the obvious and inevitable decision, recommending the publication of Coulette. And not long afterward, the poems in *The War of the Secret Agents*, with their polished manner and acerbic bite, became the Lamont Poetry Selection of 1965 of the Academy of American Poets, an important award for a first book of poems. We had good luck with the Lamont Award during my tour of duty as poetry editor, for it was also given to Adrien Stoutenburg's long narrative poem *Heroes Advise Us*.

After John Hall Wheelock retired from Scribners, I served as his editor for nearly twenty years. It was a fortunate time for me to be associated with his work, for those years were a period of flowering in his poetic life. When he died in 1978 at the age of ninety-one, Jack had been publishing poems for more than seventy years; his last book appeared posthumously, only a few months after his death. Virtually every poem he wrote had at least its starting point, I believe, in East Hampton, Long Island, in Jack's house by the sea, his birthplace, which he so loved.

John Hall Wheelock at work offered a striking illustration of the immense service that memory can afford a writer. When I spoke of memory in connection with C. P. Snow, I had in mind both its function as a source and as a means of retaining the product of the imagination. In that second function, memory acts as usefully as a pen or a typewriter, and Wheelock employed it to a degree that was awesome. He did not write down a word of a poem until the poem had been revised and had reached its final condition in his head. Moreover, Jack had the habit of carrying in his memory three or four poems in various stages of revision, the poems all different from one another in length and meter. In this fashion he worked with them; the actual "writing" amounted to no more than a clerical chore. All of Jack's poems remained permanently fixed in his memory. And he could recite not only his own work but also most of classical English poetry.

Like other poets, Jack concerned himself with the design of his book. Unlike the others, he knew the inside of publishing, and particularly the inside of Scribners. This could have caused some embarrassment for me, his editor, but he would never allow such a thing to happen. Jack Wheelock was surely the most courteous man I've ever known. His style went beyond ordinary good manners: James Jones, who was fond of Jack (and applied Jack's slouch hat and his courtesy to Bob French in *Some Came Running*), called the quality "gentle-manliness." It gave Jack a somewhat old-fashioned manner, behind which could be discerned a sly, even impish, sense of humor. From the humor came his delightful, playful "light" poems. I can remember so well, in my first days at Scribners, seeing Jack in Max Perkins' office and the two of them laughing quietly together. I would have given a lot to know what they were up to.

The poems of Jack Wheelock's old age became darker and yet serene. Their music gained a noble sound, a grandeur.

11

Singularity

The manuscript marked by singularity has always attracted me. I have been drawn to books that seem to defy classification and speak in an unfamiliar voice. This attraction can become troublesome and misleading, I have found out, and it has been necessary for me to learn caution. The crucial lesson is that the appearance of originality can prove to be freakishness. But I'm certain that the reverse of my inclination is even more dangerous. The reverse means the quick dismissal of any work that looks difficult and strange, that will not fit into a category. These books challenge an editor to recognize their genuineness.

One of them I vividly recall was the manuscript of a novel called *Crazy in Berlin*, by Thomas Berger, which came to me in 1957. At the time, Tom Berger was doing some free-lance copy edit-

ing for Scribners—exacting work which he carried
out superbly well. He and his wife Jean lived near
us in the village of Piermont, and so I saw enough
of him to know that he had been writing a novel
for three or four years. Tom Berger is a big, smiling man with a mild and cheerful manner that I
think it would be correct to call misleading. The
fruitless entertainment of trying to perceive the nature of a man's writing from his manner would
prove particularly futile with Tom Berger.

Crazy in Berlin astonished and at first baffled me.
It introduces Thomas Berger's hero-of-sorts Carlo
Reinhart, a massive and good-hearted young man
but a notable bumbler. He is an American soldier
stationed in Berlin during the occupation, surrounded by a group of bizarre characters, each of
whom has a hand in the shaping of Carlo. So the
novel has a literary classification, if one is wanted;
it is a *bildung roman*. What made trouble for me at
the outset were the peculiarities of the prose—ironic,
outrageous, dense and packed and sometimes
gnarled. As I began to find my ease with the book,
I recognized how highly individual it was, as did
other readers at Scribners, but we all saw that
Crazy in Berlin offered difficulties. One editor
urged that the author be persuaded to simplify the
most knotted sentences. But then I discovered that

Tom had deliberately sought this characteristic in the prose; he was slyly aping German syntax. We did limber up some of the most elaborately Germanic sentences, but we made only minor alterations, for Tom had his purpose, however arcane, and it had to be protected. I might add that the author stood quite ready to protect it.

I have heard Tom Berger express his delight in the resources of the American language, and his fiction supplies the evidence of his relish. It is a relish typical of comic stylists. In Berger's assaults on the contemporary scene (on the medieval scene, for that matter), nothing pleases him more than to seize hold of a trendy attitude or a taken-for-granted commonplace. He turns them upside down. His pleasure in his work can be seen in his dazzling shifts from formal prose to the vernacular, from the abstruse to the scatalogical. I think Berger might agree with a remark on style by T. E. Hulme. "All styles," Hulme said, "are only means of subduing the reader."

Thomas Berger is best known for *Little Big Man*, but in my own view his principal achievement rests in the three novels about Carlo Reinhart —*Crazy in Berlin* (1958), *Reinhart in Love*, and *Vital Parts*. The first two we published at Scribners. I am especially fond of *Reinhart in*

Love, the most genial one, and I think it offers the best elementary education in the ways and means of Thomas Berger. Here is the opening page:

"In a shed of unpainted boards, a kind of swollen privy, on a compound of like structures in a field of dirty snow somewhere in Indiana, an anonymous major, after an eleventh-hour pitch for the Regular Army or at least the Reserve, bade goodbye to thirty-odd soldiers—among whom was Corporal Carlo Reinhart, 15302320, the oddest of the lot, take it as you would: clinically: his last six months' service had been as patient in the neuropsychiatric wards of sundry military hospitals abroad and at home; emotionally: as near as he could tell, he was the only man ever released from the U. S. Army who was sorry to go; legally: the official typist had printed an error on his discharge certificate. Instead of having been born in 1924 as he had always assumed, he was but four years old; according to the War Department he had sprung from that first imprisonment in 1942, and there were all manner of officers' signatures to prove it and perhaps even confine him in Leavenworth if two months hence he applied for some deserved privilege in his authentic person of twenty-one.

"So, although now a civilian, he reported his problem to the major with nostalgic military courtesy, and got for his pains a rather wry direction to the typing building. The other jokers all rushed out towards the camp gate and the waiting bus, not having a minute to lose in getting back to brown-nose their civilian bosses. Reinhart was unfair because he didn't know any of them; the shitty thing about a separation center was that you were there for only three days of signing papers (which were sometimes faulty!) and everybody arrived slightly hostile to one another—already halfway back to civil society."

Thomas Berger's voice gave notice of a new tone in fiction. Variations of it can be heard now in the work of a number of young writers. When strain enters the tone, it becomes tiresome, and even Berger, with all his virtuosity, has not entirely avoided it. But, by and large, he has an easy command of what he does. With the writing equipment in his possession and the abundance of absurdities within his view, he ought to keep busy all his life.

These singular, defiantly unclassifiable books become all the more difficult for an editor when he is involved in them as they grow—as works in progress. At its simplest, coping with a work in progress is filled with uncertainty. The first fifty pages do not necessarily establish the quality of the next fifty. I think that out of experience an editor develops a sense of when a book is going well, or badly; but his confidence in himself will surely weaken when the writer appears to be taking an unpredictable course.

That was so for me with Richard Elman's novel *An Education in Blood* (1971). He had already published his remarkable trilogy about the Holocaust—*The 28th Day of Elul, Lilo's Diary,* and *The Reckoning.* But the new novel he proposed differed radically in nature. Elman found the idea for *An Education in Blood* in a famous California murder case of more than thirty years ago, in which a man named David Lamson had been accused and convicted three times of the murder of his wife, and then, at last, declared innocent. Lamson had himself written a book about the experience—*Whirlpool,* published by Scribners.

Elman used the actual case simply as raw material. His novel concerns a young radical journalist who comes to Los Angeles determined to confront the man once accused of murder and to penetrate the truth. *An Education in Blood* consists of a sequence of increasingly intense and disturbing exchanges between the two men as they goad each other and thereby reveal themselves.

I read the novel as it grew, in sections. The

power soon became evident, and so did the possibilities; but I could not see the direction, and I think Richard himself continually had to make choices between alternatives opened up by the story as it progressed. Particularly for a man of Richard Elman's intensity and compulsive drive, the writing of that novel must have often been torment. And I could not do very much to lessen it. I could say to Richard that what he had written interested and moved me, but I could not give him the more valuable assurance that he was on the right track. I did not know.

There was an ultimate moment, however, in which I did serve the novel well. Shortly after he had finished it, Richard called me up; he said that he had just burned the manuscript. I was able to remind him that I had a Xerox copy. I persuaded him to accept the fact that his book existed.

Dick Elman's personality, from what I have said about him, may seem rather somber. That is inaccurate. An intense man, he has also a persistent sense of comic absurdity, and he brings a good deal of high spirits into life around him. Some years ago, when I was about to go into the hospital for a minor operation, I received a going-in present from him, with a card saying, "For consolation." The present proved to be a small red book—*Quotations from Chairman Mao Tse-tung*.

I'm reminded of another episode, for which Richard can be given only indirect credit. In this case, Elman had gone into the hospital and he had left my wife Jean and me in charge of his pet white female dove—Snowflake by name. We let the bird fly around our apartment from time to time, and on one of these occasions, while I was talking on the phone, Jean noticed something I was unaware of; Snowflake had perched on my head. The fact is that the person I was talking to was Roberta Pryor, Elman's literary agent, and we must have been discussing her client. While I completed my conversation with Roberta and Jean attempted to control her laughter, Snowflake, remaining seated on my head, did the inevitable. She gently shat. The editorial life carries many risks.

Everything about *Miss MacIntosh, My Darling*, by Marguerite Young, seemed to be without precedent. For years it was surely the best known literary work in progress in the United States. Portions of it appeared in various literary publications, like *Tiger's Eye*, and Marguerite Young received several fellowships. She had lived in Iowa, in Rome, in New York City, and always she wrote; but as time

passed, quite a number of people concluded that
the book would never be finished. This conclusion
arose from a serious miscalculation of Marguerite
Young. In 1964—more than seventeen years after
Max Perkins had taken the book under contract—a
beautifully typed manuscript of 3,449 pages arrived at Scribners, the finished work. After Perkins' death, the editorial inheritance had moved to
Jack Wheelock, then to Wallace Meyer, and then
to me, who knew the least about the book. I began
to read it during my vacation on Nantucket.

Miss MacIntosh, My Darling may be the longest
novel in American literature, containing as it does
more than six hundred thousand words. More important is the fact that it is a prodigious demon-
stration of lyrical, rhetorical virtuosity. As I read
deeper into that manuscript, I did so with a growing wonder at the poetic, incantatory eloquence
that never wavers in its certainty. To find a similar
prose texture it may be necessary to go back to Sir
Thomas Browne. And yet Marguerite has also
given her book moments of Dickensian realism, as
downright and comic as Miss MacIntosh herself,
who hails from What Cheer, Iowa. From the abundance of interplaying themes, one emerges as central: the insistent, repeating question of what is real
and what is dream. Or, as Marguerite Young her-

self has put it: "What shall we do when, fleeing from illusion, we are confronted by illusion?"

Not long after she had finished her book, Marguerite wrote me a long letter about it. She wrote it as she traveled by subway to the class she taught at Fordham and the letter was headed, "(*D train!*)." Here are portions of it:

"Indeed, it is a picaresque psychological novel—a novel of the road and of the human spirit in its search for identity, reality, truth, love in a world of nightmare and illusion and dream like those mountain fogs and mists. And what is reality? I think I wanted to say that the dream or the illusion cannot be dismissed as the mere flotsam of creation. The dream is the reality. We live by our illusions as we die by them.

"Many people have asked how much of the novel I had in mind on that fateful Tuesday morning I began it—having never intended to create a novel then at all—having told myself that I would wait to write a novel when I was old and had reached the grandeur of age and wisdom. Quite by chance, because of a publisher's venture, I began the novel then when I was young and wrote every day until I was old. From the first day—and I had only thought of it forty-eight hours—I knew the general structure of the novel—a psychological journey—the major characters from the first to the last—from the opium lady and Miss MacIntosh and Mr. Spitzer clear to the hangman and the stone-deaf man, the very final scene, and the over-all content of the novel, that it would be musical and imagistic and psychological, that the movement and imagery would dramatize the inner life, make visible that which might be invisible if one were not discerning.

"Almost nothing in my novel is invented—in fact, I should say that nothing is. Everything, the wildest situation, was *observed* by me, known by me, my motto being that truth is certainly stranger than fiction. Sometimes a wild event occurred, as if in affirmation, after I had written it. Thus you may remember that Miss MacIntosh walks into the sea quite naked except that she carries a black umbrella and wears black gloves. Sometime after this, a man walked naked into the sea off Long Island except for black gloves—committing suicide. Now what do the black gloves mean? I think we may know at an unconscious level if not a conscious level (which is never necessary). The black gloves are a symbol of guilt and loneliness. Hence these are the gloves which Miss MacIntosh would have worn to her marriage with the Bible salesman . . . Now the reader does not have to know these things consciously as I do. The point is that they are not mere whim or decoration. They have a psychological origin and bring a disturbing revelation, make for revelation.

"Illumination, the reader's *recognition* and *identification*. Why? Because all of us are lonely, and all of us yearn for the sea as the child yearns for the mother—or as Miss MacIntosh yearns for her hair, her hair of illusion. She is bald. She is more male than female . . .

"Of all the characters, I feel Miss MacIntosh is most nearly imaginary—perhaps because the lives of spinsters are so often tentative and amorphous. I made her a descendant of John Knox and a lost Stuart because I am a descendant (as were James Boswell, Herman Melville, and many other great writers of our language. Lord Byron, for example.) She is a Presbyterian—a Puritan "fall of man" character in the opium paradise of ancient pagan or Hebrew or Catholic imagery, illusion, dream. Her quarrel with the Emperor Constantine who changed the calendar was my grandmother's quarrel. Mr. Bonebreaker, name and all, was an old Bible scholar I knew in my childhood. But actually, the novel is not autobiographical—far more material coming from the News and Mirror and Time magazine! than from my life's experience.

"I think that the novel is an exploration of many psychologies—the psychology of opium addiction.

"The psychology of twins . . . dual or alternating personality as old as Poe and older.

"The psychology of baldness and hair—Samson, Absalom—the psychology of the suffrage movement—the psychology of reincarnation . . .

"I wanted this to be an epic—to tell something of truly fantastic American life! Far from the dull neutrality of Main Street and the supermarket! Our real Arabian Nights America!"

Marguerite had lived for some years in an apartment on Bleecker Street, surrounded by hundreds of angels and dolls and even a carrousel horse. She was a familiar figure in the Village neighborhood, particularly at her local drugstore, which she regarded with the affection an English writer gives to his favorite pub. While *Miss MacIntosh* was in production—a time filled with perils—Marguerite became a frequent visitor at Scribners, arriving with her habitually pleasant expression and wrapped in one of her capes. In conversation, her sentences take on a rhythm and verbal richness that make you realize how much she is her book. Her eloquence flows as naturally as common speech.

The preparation of *Miss MacIntosh, My Darling* proceeded in its unprecedented fashion, offering

me a new crisis almost every week—all of them
bearing on the vast size of the book. The reading of
proof alone was a staggering job, which Eleanor
Sullivan supervised at the Scribner end and which
Marguerite coped with, on Bleecker Street, most
efficiently. Finally there existed a massive volume
of twelve hundred pages, set in a type that was
possible to read. We had somehow done it. When
the first books arrived from the printer, Marguerite
inscribed a copy to me as "angel at the helm."
Then she asked me to inscribe a copy to her—something I had never been asked to do.

On publication, in 1965, *Miss MacIntosh, My
Darling* was received by the *Times Book Review*
in a fashion that Marguerite and I, certainly, will
not ever forget. The reviewer was William Goyen,
and he called the novel "a work of stunning magni-
tude and beauty . . . one of the most arresting literary achievements of our last twenty years . . . a
masterwork." That set things going; the huge book
was soon being talked about, and selling. Marguerite became in demand on television; indeed, she
appeared so many times, she told me delightedly,
that she would have to join a union. Celebratory
parties took place, among them a party of memorable proportions at Ruth Stephan's home in Greenwich, Connecticut, to which people were brought

from the city in busloads and were greeted at the door with champagne. Anaïs Nin was there, looking beautiful. The lawn at the rear of the house swept down to a lake where a gondola plied in the dusk. Two angels passed among the guests. (The angels proved to be disguised members of the Scribner publicity department.)

While these excitements went on, _Miss MacIntosh_ continued to receive the frequently confused attentions of the reviewers. They praised and they ridiculed. The supporters included Anaïs Nin and Mark Van Doren, whose comment on the novel seems to me the most apt of them all. He said: "Marguerite Young's eloquence has no parallel among the novelists of our time. It comes in rivers and whirlwinds, and carries on its back, along with bits of unidentifiable matter, masses of rich and surprising life."

12

The Manuscript

*E*very book editor has started out by reading manuscripts. As he advances in his education and in his responsibilities, he must puzzle his way through a variety of duties, which have been unfavorably compared with the functions of a psychiatrist, and an errand boy, and a plantation overseer. In all this, an editor may lose sight of a simple fact, that the manuscript remains immovably central.

I think there are three signal moments in an editor's working life compared with which the many dreary jobs and frustrations seem trivial. The first of these moments comes with finding a manuscript that is animated with a life particularly its own. Only someone who has worked in a publishing house can have a sense of how inexorably the manuscripts flood in, from everywhere, as if every household in the world had a typewriter. And so, if he is to survive, an editor, it seems to me, must have one deeply rooted trait—the ability to pick up each new manuscript with curiosity and hope. If he has that, his day will come, sooner or later.

Much later, it often seems. The flow of manuscripts brings so much failed work—so many earnest, ponderous efforts, and smart posturings, and little flashes of talent that die out before the book ends. It is easy for the manuscript reader to become depressed, especially because he can recognize that many of these failures represent high purpose and hard work. But then the unexpected, hoped-for moment comes—the manuscript with the indescribable and yet immediately evident property of life that signifies a real writer. Can the writer sustain the vivifying quality of the first pages? I clearly recall my increasing pleasure and confidence when, twenty years ago, I read into the manuscript of Sue Kaufman's first novel, *The Happy Summer Days*, which Carol Brandt, the agent, had sent me. Just as firm in my memory is my bewildered curiosity as to what Thomas Berger would do on the next page, and then the next, of *Crazy in Berlin*.

Reading a manuscript draws an editor into a contact with the author quite different from a reader's relationship with a published book. When a piece of writing goes into type, a change results.

Jim Jones told me that this was a lot of mystical nonsense, but he was wrong. The printing process does make its effect; good or bad, the piece of writing now assumes an air of permanence. And moreover, on publication, a book becomes a public matter. But the manuscript just discovered may be undergoing its first exposure when you, the editor, read it. You have joined the author in an odd, intimate association between two strangers.

Once having encountered the writer in his work, you are inevitably curious about the shape of the actual person. The meeting between editor and writer becomes the second of the three moments I have spoken of. And it may be a meeting filled with unexpressed complications. Perhaps the author of a first book has heard some of the prevalent tales of horror about publishers; he will then arrive encased in suspicion and determined to protect his work from corruption. On the extreme other hand, the author may be in an incoherent state, stunned by the fact that some unknown person—and a publisher!—claims to like his book. He may sit in virtual silence at the meeting, smiling a little foolishly. In either condition, with guard up or struck silent, the writer, in his real self, will remain out of reach.

To be sure, I have offered two extreme situations, neither one common. But variations between these extremes are common enough. What is apt to happen is that the author will arrive with conflicting feelings of worry and hope—the dark suspicion that he must keep his wits about him and the readiness to be joyful. If the editor manages to allay worry (at least temporarily) and to transmute the author's hopefulness into the beginning of trust, he will have done his best. It may be that the biggest accomplishment he can expect will consist in persuading the writer that here is somebody who actually appears to understand what his book is about.

Max Perkins spoke in his letters of "the motive for fiction" and of how it was often misunderstood in its seriousness of intention. While a writer and an editor sit, perhaps uneasily, in their first meeting, the editor will be attempting to get at the motive, the impelling force, in this stranger. He will gain no more than a sense of it. In fact, if the writer should announce a portentous statement of purpose, that will be cause for doubts. But an editor has got to look for reassuring indications that, having found a book, he has also found a writer—a writer with the indispensable supply of energy and bullheadedness. In the end, that first meeting between editor and writer may not come to much, but it will have been invested with an excitement that neither is likely to forget. I can remember nothing of what was said the first time James Jones came to see me at Scribners. But I do still have an impression of his general look—friendly, uneasy, but determined.

The third occasion I think of as a high moment is the publication of the book. It is a time of great strain, the approach of publication day; the author jitters, or drinks too much, or pretends he doesn't care, fooling no one. As for the editor, I am sure that many of them have had my persistent experience, the total loss of objectivity. While the book exists only in manuscript, it remains open to revision and the editor therefore maintains a degree of critical detachment. But that stops on publication day, and the editor becomes as violently partisan as his nature permits. His job is to calm the author, but, just the same, the first unkind word from a reviewer may cause him to react with unreasonable heat.

Once in a while, the great thing happens. The reviewers, one after another, discover the book and hail the author. The book becomes visible everywhere, in bookstore windows and even in the hands of subway riders. It is discussed knowledgeably by people who haven't read it. All the little explosions of publicity go off. And the publisher rejoices over the dilemma of how large to make the second printing. Through these bewildering days and weeks, the writer, if the book is his first, has been going through a change within himself—from amateur to professional. The editor has had his judgment confirmed and his secret doubts silenced for good, and momentarily his ego luxuriates. But perhaps, in all his ebullience, he will be able to remember those admirable books that died very quiet deaths. They should be remembered, and with respect.

Many events in publishing may turn out to be more important than the three I have singled out, but I suspect that none will have an equal excitement. These are the three chief steps of entry into association with a writer and his career.

Having entered this far, an editor stands in danger of overestimating himself. The invigorating lift of a publishing success may very well lead the editor to feel possessive toward the writer. Fortunately for everyone, the possessiveness will not work. No editor tried harder to avoid it than Max Perkins, and yet Thomas Wolfe thought he felt it and went thundering off, having exhausted Max with his torrent of explanations. Possessiveness will not work because it implies a transcendent importance in the editorial function that simply is not true. The editor did not write the book; the author did, and what is more, he knows it. We now hear the phrase "creative editing" a good deal. Some years ago, Herbert Read wrote that "creative" was "a word to be used with discretion," and his good advice has been conspicuously unheeded. I don't believe that an editor's part in a book is a creative act. The writer performs that act.

That is not to say that an editor limits himself to correcting the spelling. Editorial work does require imagination—the imagination to see the contours of a book with something close to the author's vision. The capacity to do that makes the editor a valuable ally for any writer.

Early in this book I said that the act of writing is a lonely one. In fact, a writer lives in a peculiar and contradictory condition. He treasures his independence (sometimes to the point of egomania); he values the times of solitude necessary for his work. And yet it is often a troubled solitude, and it can grow so painful that there must be relief. That is what the editor can provide more satisfactorily, perhaps, than anyone else. Assurances of confidence from family and friends cannot wholly sustain the writer, for the simple reason that he takes for granted their uncritical, unquestioning support. In the support from an editor, a writer demands hard, critical honesty.

I suppose that as the publishing business grows in complexity, reverberating with million-dollar deals, an editor's duties will become even more multifarious and bizarre. But I cannot see how the foremost editorial responsibility can diminish—that is, the hopeful, understanding reading of a manuscript. Here is where an editor's education begins, and it is an education that never ends.

It is an odd sort of occupation to take up—reading manuscripts. The truth is that the occupation lays a claim on one's life. It might seem, then, not to be very much of a life; but since I began to read manuscripts professionally, more than forty years ago, I have not ever wanted different work, nor have I felt that work of any other kind could give me so strong a sense of purpose. When I ceased my editorial job at Scribners, I could have taken it as a release from drudgery. But instead what I did was to start at once to look around here and there for manuscripts. And quite soon they began to appear.

Burroughs Mitchell died in July 1979, but he left behind the legacy of several years' work on a lengthy historical novel set in ancient Ceylon, by Colin de Silva, which Doubleday is proud to be publishing on a forthcoming list.